Cupcake Decorating Lab

First published in the United States of America in 2013 by
Quarry Books, a member of
Quayside Publishing Group
100 Cummings Center
Suite 406-L
Beverly, Massachusetts 01915-6101
Telephone: (978) 282-9590
Fax: (978) 283-2742
www.quarrybooks.com
Visit www.Craftside.Typepad.com for a behind-the-scenes peek at our crafty world!

10 9 8 7 6 5 4 3 2 1

ISBN: 978-1-59253-831-7

Digital edition published in 2013
eISBN: 978-1-61058-767-9

Library of Congress Cataloging-in-Publication Data is available

Book Layout: *tabula rasa* graphic design, www.trgraphicdesign.com
Series Design: John Hall Design Group, www.johnhalldesign.com
Phototography: Eastwind Studio LLC
Food Styling: Brynn Keefe

Printed in China

Cupcake Decorating Lab

52 Techniques, Recipes, and Inspiring Designs for Your Favorite Sweet Treats!

Bridget Thibeault

Quarry Books
100 Cummings Center, Suite 406L
Beverly, MA 01915

quarrybooks.com • craftside.typepad.com

Contents

Introduction

AT LUNA, MY BAKERY, WE BAKE ALL OF OUR CUPCAKES, frostings, and other pastries from scratch daily using the finest ingredients. I believe in baking from scratch and eating quality, fresh ingredients and I hope this book will inspire you to do the same. However, I am also a busy mom and I understand that baking and decorating take time. This is one of the many reasons I love cupcakes. They are quick to make and much less intimidating to frost and decorate than a large cake.

This book is bursting with straightforward, fun, and creative ways to decorate cupcakes that can be used for many occasions. Some of the designs are works of art and others are sweet and simple concepts. Once you master the basics, this book will encourage you to try other "professional" techniques such as making sugar flowers, piping with royal icing, and creating a cupcake cake. There are time saving tips for working ahead on the little details and embellishments. And you'll also get excellent ideas for presenting your cupcakes in contemporary ways by using objects like shot glasses, mason jars, and espresso cups. Combine the ideas from a few of these labs to create a fabulous dessert table. Have fun with this book and enjoy the cupcakes!

Materials for Baking

Some basic materials you will need for baking cupcakes and making the recipes include standard-size cupcake pans, standard-size cupcake liners, an ice cream scoop, a mixer, mixing bowls, spatulas, a whisk, dry measuring cups, a liquid measuring cup, measuring spoons, a mesh sifter, sheet trays, and a medium saucepan.

Materials for Basic Decorating

The materials you will need to decorate the cupcakes include a 4" (10 cm) offset spatula; 14"–18" (36–46 cm) pastry bags; small craft scissors; pastry tips (Ateco #806 or #826, Ateco #804, #2 round, #3, Witon #401 or #79 or Ateco #81, Ateco #234, Wilton #1M or #2D, Ateco #21 or #30, Ateco #897, Ateco #070, Wilton or Ateco #18); gel or paste food coloring; toothpicks; small microwaveable bowls; edible decorations such as sprinkles, sanding sugar, edible pearls, and multi-colored nonpareils; a small parchment piping bag; small paintbrushes; parchment paper or wax paper; assorted sizes of mixing bowls; tweezers; a paring knife; and a cutting board.

The sugar flower and fondant supplies include a fondant rolling pin, round cookie cutters, fluted round cookie cutters, a pastry brush, colored fondant and gumpaste, a wheel pastry cutter or pizza cutter, stencils, luster or petal dust, 1"–3" (2.5–7.6 cm) flower cutters, a foam pad, a ball tool, an egg carton or aluminum foil, a flower mold, a leaf veiner, and edible glue or egg white.

Materials for Specific Labs

Additional supplies that are specific to labs include a surfboard cookie cutter, a small ice cream scoop, a fondue pot, skewers, oven-safe espresso cups, 2 food-safe squeeze bottles, sugar cubes, a rocks glass, a sleeveless dress cookie cutter, a jumbo cupcake pan and liners, sugar flowers, shot glasses, mini cupcake pans and liners, mason jars, push pop containers, a mini cake mold, a metal rack, a ladle, silicone cupcake molds or porcelain ramekins, a roasting pan, a silicone fondant mold, an impression mat, rubber stamps, 3" (7.6 cm) terra cotta pots, and a nonstick mini doughnut mold.

Icing Basics

A CUPCAKE IS A DELICIOUS TREAT and often does not need elaborate decoration. A simple swirl or shiny glaze can be just the right touch to brighten up a party, wedding, or dessert table. Add sprinkles for a festive finishing touch.

In this unit you will learn basic icing techniques using a variety of frostings. These cupcakes are wonderful as is, or can serve as a nice starting point for more ornate designs.

UNIT

1

frosting with Buttercream

- cupcakes
- buttercream (see recipe on page 133)
- 4" (10 cm) offset spatula

There are many ways to frost a cupcake with buttercream—there really is no wrong way. With practice, you can develop your own method and decide what works best. In this lab you will learn a basic technique for frosting with a small offset spatula. And if you are not completely satisfied with your results, sprinkles are a nice finishing touch and can hide any imperfections.

Tip:

Use an ice cream scoop to get a nice round dollop of buttercream on top of each cupcake. Plus all your cupcakes will have equal amounts of frosting!

Let's Go!

(A) *dollop buttercream in center*

1. Place a large dollop of buttercream in the center of the cupcake. (See A.)
2. Using the offset spatula, swirl the buttercream in a clockwise motion all the way around the cupcake. (See B.)
3. Cut back in a counterclockwise motion while moving in toward the center of the cupcake. (See C.)

(B) *swirl in a clockwise motion*

(C) *cut back in toward the center*

Piping with Buttercream

- cupcake
- buttercream (see recipe on page 133)
- 14"–18" (36–46 cm) pastry bag
- large round plain pastry or star tip, such as Ateco #806 or #826
- scissors
- spatula or spoon

Piping buttercream in a swirl on top of a cupcake creates a gourmet look. You can use a round or star pastry tip—experiment with different sizes. Practice first on a piece of parchment or wax paper, and then scoop up the frosting and reuse.

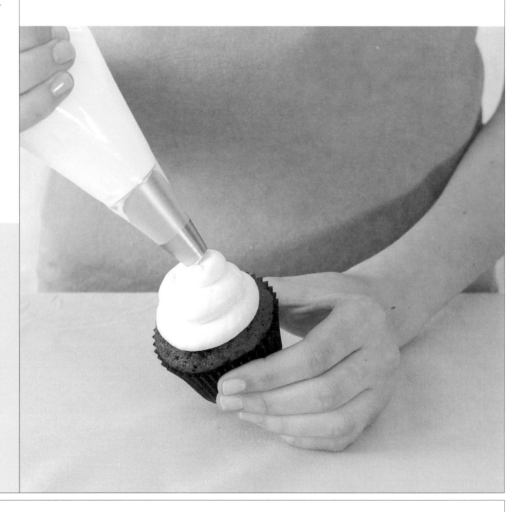

Filling a Pastry Bag

Make a "C" with your hand. Fold the pastry bag edges over your hand and fill. Twist the top of the bag to close, securing with a twist tie or plastic wrap so the frosting does not squeeze out the back end. To secure with plastic wrap, twist a piece of plastic wrap into a rope, and then tie it into a knot around the bag to close.

Let's Go!

(A) *scoop frosting into bag*

(B) *pipe a circle*

(C) *continue to pipe on top of the base circle*

1. Cut a small hole in the tip of the pastry bag large enough for the pastry tip to pop out. Place the tip into the bag.

2. Scoop the buttercream frosting into the pastry bag, filling the bag halfway. (See A.)

3. Hold the bag vertically at a ninety-degree angle, about ¼" (6 mm) from the center of a cupcake. Pipe the frosting in a clockwise motion, moving out toward the edge of the cupcake and forming a complete circle. (See B.)

4. Continue to pipe over the base circle, moving in toward the center. (See C.)

5. Release the pressure on the bag, and quickly pull away at an angle for a clean break. If you pull away straight up, you will have a peak on top of your frosting. (See D.)

(D) *release pressure and pull away*

LAB 3 Tinting Buttercream

You'll Need

- buttercream (see recipe on page 133)
- gel or paste food coloring
- small microwaveable bowl
- spatula or spoon
- toothpicks

Food Coloring

Do not use liquid food coloring. You can find gel or paste food coloring at your local craft or cake-decorating store. The color is much more intense and the taste is more subtle. The gel or paste also contains less water so it does not affect the consistency of your buttercream. Gel food coloring blends more easily than paste. If you can find squeeze bottles, they are less messy.

Buttercream is very easy to tint but there are a few tips to consider to achieve the best color. I try to keep things as natural as possible when baking, but when you need a brightly colored buttercream you will have to use food coloring. In this lab you will learn how to use less food coloring by heating the food coloring and buttercream together to intensify the end color.

Let's Go!

(A) add gel food color to buttercream

(B) stir to combine

1. Put a dollop of buttercream into the microwaveable bowl. Use a toothpick to add the desired amount of the gel color. (See A.) Microwave the mixture for ten seconds. Alternatively, you can melt the mixture over a double boiler.

2. The colored buttercream will be liquid in consistency. Stir to combine. The color should be much more intense than your desired color. (See B.)

3. Add the colored buttercream to the larger bowl of white buttercream; stir to combine. (See C.)

4. If you desire a brighter color, repeat the process. If you want a less intense color, add white buttercream to the colored buttercream.

5. Your buttercream may be too soft for piping due to its heat. Place it in the refrigerator for a few minutes to set, or make the colors in advance to avoid this issue.

(C) add to bowl of white buttercream

Striping with Buttercream

- cupcakes
- 2 colors of buttercream (see recipe on page 133; pink and green shown)
- 14"–18" (35.6–45.7 cm) pastry bag fitted with a large star tip, such as Ateco #826

Colorful buttercream will brighten up any cupcake. In this lab you will learn how to stripe buttercream with two or more colors in a piping bag. This technique can also be used with shades of one color for realistic looking flowers, leaves, and other designs.

Tip

Create multicolor stripes by adding thinner stripes of various colors inside the pastry bag.

Let's Go!

(A) *slide one color into bag*

(B) *slide the second color into the bag*

(C) *begin piping*

1. Slide the first color of buttercream into the pastry bag along one side, moving from the tip to the end. Do not let the buttercream touch the opposite side of the bag. (See A.)
2. Slide the second color of buttercream along the opposite side of the bag. (See B.)
3. Seal the bag and pipe the buttercream onto a cupcake in a clockwise motion, moving out toward the edge of the cupcake and forming a complete circle. (See C and D.) Continue to pipe over the base circle, moving in toward the center to add more buttercream.
4. Release the pressure on the bag, and quickly pull away at an angle for a clean break. If you pull away straight up, you will have a peak on top of your frosting.

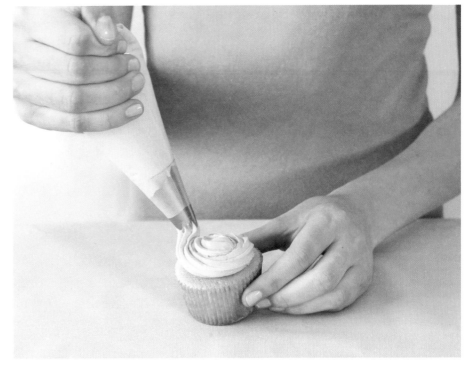

(D) *complete circle of icing*

Chocolate Ganache Glaze

- cupcakes
- ganache (see recipe on page 135)
- melted white chocolate
- sprinkles or edible confetti (hearts shown)
- 4" (10 cm) offset spatula
- small parchment piping bag

Ganache is a favorite among chocolate lovers. This shiny glaze creates a sophisticated cupcake and would be ideal with a single raspberry on top or white chocolate drizzle. Our "love" cupcake is a perfect treat for an anniversary or Valentine's Day celebration.

Tip

Chocolate must be at the correct temperature and consistency for writing—not too runny or too stiff. Practice writing on parchment paper. Decorating gel tubes are a good substitute.

Taking it Further

For a different look, chill the ganache or let it sit at room temperature until it is thick enough to pipe. Scoop the ganache into a pastry bag and pipe according to instructions in Lab 2 (page 12). This technique can be seen in Lab 27 (page 72).

Let's Go!

(A) *dip cupcake into ganache*

(B) *allow excess to drip off*

1. Make ganache and use while still warm. If ganache is cold or at room temperature, heat ganache in a microwave or double boiler until warm and fluid.

2. If necessary, trim a cupcake top so that it has a smooth or slightly domed shape.

3. Dip the cupcake top into the ganache. (See A.) Allow the excess ganache to drip off the cupcake for a few seconds. (See B.)

4. Turn the cupcake upright to set. Smooth out any imperfections with the offset spatula. (See C.)

5. Fill the piping bag with warm white chocolate, and pipe a design. (See D.)

6. Sprinkle with edible decorations.

(C) *smooth out any imperfections*

(D) *pipe design with white chocolate*

Flooding with Icing

- cupcakes
- royal icing or fruit glaze; runny consistency (see recipes on pages 136 and 135)
- fresh fruit garnish; optional
- 4" (10 cm) offset spatula

Flooding with icing is a very simple technique that gives a nice smooth finish to your cupcake. It is not your traditional buttercream cupcake, but you can always fill your cupcakes with a delicious surprise inside—buttercream, jam, ganache, or lemon curd.

Tip

If you don't want your icing to run to the edges, thicken it with powdered sugar until the icing holds its shape, and then spread it on your cupcake.

Let's Go!

(A) *test that your icing is runny*

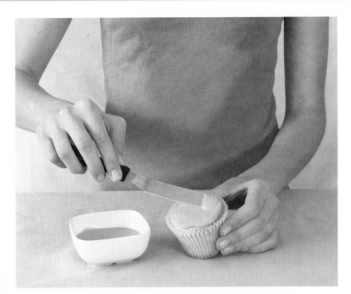

(B) *spread icing on cupcake*

1. Make sure your icing is runny enough to fall off your spatula so the icing will settle smoothly on the cupcake. (See A.)
2. Starting at the center, spread icing onto a cupcake with the spatula. (See B.)
3. Spread the icing to the edge but not over the liner. (See C.)
4. Garnish with fresh fruit, if desired.
5. Alternatively, you can dip the cupcake in the icing like in Lab 5 (page 18).

(C) *spread icing to edge, but not over liner*

Sugared
Fruits & Flowers

IN THIS UNIT YOU WILL LEARN candying and sugaring techniques using fresh fruits and edible flowers. Their natural beauty and amazing taste make them lovely garnishes for cupcakes. To keep things seasonal, we have recipes for both summer berries and winter citrus. The flowers can be made months in advance to showcase all year long.

UNIT

2

Sugared Berries

- frosted cupcakes
- berries (raspberries, blueberries, and blackberries shown)
- superfine sugar
- egg white
- toothpick
- small paintbrush
- parchment or waxed paper

Berries are gorgeous and don't need extra adornment when they are in season. But when they are essential to many desserts throughout the rest of the year, we often have to glaze or macerate them in sugar to bring out their flavor. In this lab, you will learn to sugar berries for a festive new look.

Tip

To make your own superfine sugar, or castor sugar, process granulated sugar in your food processor fitted with a metal blade for 1–2 minutes. The sugar should be powdery and much finer.

Let's Go!

(A) insert toothpick

(B) brush with egg white

(C) sprinkle berry with sugar

1. Spear a berry with a toothpick. (See A.)
2. Brush the berry with a thin layer of egg white. (See B.)
3. Lightly sprinkle the berry with sugar while rotating the fruit. (See C.)
4. Continue to rotate the berry and coat with sugar.
5. Let the berries dry at least 30 minutes on parchment or waxed paper.
6. Arrange the garnish on your favorite cupcake.

Sugar Your Favorite Fruits

Small fruits look best when sugared, such as Seckel pears, plums, grapes, and lady apples. Brush them with egg white and roll in sugar. Use these larger fruits to decorate cakes, or cluster them in a pretty bowl as a centerpiece.

- cupcakes
- colored buttercream (see recipe on page 133; orange, red, and yellow shown)
- white sanding sugar
- Tootsie Roll candies
- fondant leaves
- 4" (10 cm) offset spatula
- scissors

A basket of fruit-inspired cupcakes is a lovely addition to a picnic lunch. In this lab you will make peach cupcakes, but this technique can be used for any round fruit. And if you want to add a little sparkle to any cupcake, use the method of sugaring the buttercream as explained below.

Tip
Spearmint jelly leaves make a good substitute for the fondant leaves.

Let's Go!

(A) add yellow buttercream

(B) swirl in red buttercream

(C) dip cupcake in sugar

1. Frost half of a cupcake with orange buttercream.
2. Frost the other half of the cupcake with yellow buttercream. (See A.)
3. Add a dollop of red buttercream and swirl the colors together for a natural peach look. (See B.)
4. Dip the top of the cupcake in the sanding sugar to coat. (See C.)
5. Cut a Tootsie Roll in quarters, lengthwise for the stems.
6. Place one stem and one fondant leaf on each cupcake. (See D.)

Taking It Further

Make a basket of mixed fruit using the appropriate colored frostings for apples, peaches, plums, oranges, and lemons.

(D) add stem and leaf to cupcake

Candied Flowers

- frosted cupcakes
- edible flowers (nontoxic and organic) such as violets, violas, chamomile flowers, pansies, and roses
- 1 egg white
- superfine sugar
- scissors
- tweezers
- small paintbrush
- parchment or waxed paper

Candied or crystallized flowers are a lovely garnish for teatime cupcakes or a ladies' shower or luncheon. This is a great do-ahead project because candied flowers will keep for months. Be sure to request nontoxic and organic flowers at your florist or market. Local farmers' markets are a good source for these flowers, or they should be able to give you a recommendation of where to find them.

Storing Candied Flowers

Candied flowers will keep up to three months if stored properly. Be sure the flowers are completely dry before packaging, which could take two to three days depending on the size of the flower. Store in single layers on parchment paper in an airtight container at room temperature.

Let's Go!

1. Trim the flower stems, leaving ½" (1.5 cm) attached to the flower.
2. Dilute the egg white with a couple drops of water.
3. Hold a flower with the tweezers, and brush the entire flower with a thin layer of egg white. (See A.)
4. Sprinkle the flower with some sugar; shake to remove excess sugar. (See B.)
5. Place the flower on a piece of parchment paper and let dry a few hours.
6. Arrange the flowers on your favorite cupcakes.

OPPOSITE: These cupcakes were frosted with a thick royal icing (page 136).

(A) brush flower with egg white

(B) sprinkle flower with sugar

Candied Citrus Slices

- frosted cupcakes
- citrus fruits such as lemons, limes, oranges, and kumquats
- sugar
- sanding sugar

There are many ways to cut citrus to be candied—all are beautiful and delicious. Candied citrus looks fancy but is simple to make and keeps for a long time. In this lab you will store the citrus in its own citrus syrup, and use it as a cupcake garnish. However, you can dry the slices and roll them in sugar for a drier, chewier version.

Tips

- Use extra syrup for brushing on cupcakes, cake layers, and flavoring drinks.
- For a dried citrus slice, instead of storing the candied fruit in simple syrup, let the citrus dry on a rack and then store in an airtight container.

Let's Go!

1. Slice a whole citrus fruit crosswise into ¼" (6 mm)-thick circles. Remove the seeds as you see them.

2. To reduce the bitterness, place the slices in a saucepan with enough cold water to cover. Bring the water to a boil, drain, and repeat. Remove the slices from the pan.

3. In the same pan and using enough liquid to cover the slices, bring equal parts sugar and water to a boil. Once the sugar is dissolved, add the fruit slices back to the pan. Simmer the slices in the simple syrup at least 30 minutes. Remove the pan to a rack and let the contents cool.

4. Store the slices in the simple syrup in the refrigerator. Drain the syrup from the fruit before using.

5. For decorating, use a variety of techniques. Edge lime halves and kumquats in sanding sugar. (See A.) Cut a slit in an orange slice and twist it like a rose. (See B.) Place candied citrus fruit on cupcakes.

Citrus Curls

Remove long strips of zest with a vegetable peeler, avoiding the pith. Slice into ¼" (6 mm)-wide strips with a paring knife. Proceed, beginning with step 2 of the instructions.

(A) edge in sugar

(B) cut slit and twist like a rose

Fondant

ROLLED FONDANT IS A SUGAR DOUGH that for years was used mostly for wedding cake decorating. Recently, fondant has become very popular for basic cake decorations, cookies, and cupcakes. It includes gelatin, which keeps the dough pliable, and it can be rolled out, or sculpted into shapes and figures. Fondant is not difficult to make but I prefer to buy a nice quality fondant that tastes good and is easy to work with. In this unit, we will learn how to cover cupcakes with fondant, use molds and impression mats, and decorate fondant cupcake toppers.

UNIT

3

Covering with Fondant

- cupcakes
- fondant
- cornstarch
- buttercream (see recipe on page 133)
- fondant rolling pin
- round cookie cutter, approximately 2¼" (5.7 cm)
- pastry brush or paintbrush
- 4" (10 cm) offset spatula

Fondant is a wonderful material for covering cake or cupcakes. It lets you start your creation with a nice, clean, flat surface—like an artist's canvas. From there the options are endless. And children love the chewy marshmallow-like texture and flavor! Two examples of the types of designs you can make with fondant are shown below: The top images are from Lab 12 (see page 36) and the bottom from Lab 22 (see page 60).

Taking it Further

Instead of buttercream, try using ganache or jam underneath the fondant. If the jam is lumpy, thin it with a few drops of hot water to make it easy to spread.

Let's Go!

(A) *dust with cornstarch*

(B) *roll the fondant*

(D) *spread buttercream on cupcake*

(C) *cut a fondant circle*

(E) *place on cupcake and smooth*

1. Knead the fondant until pliable. Dust the work surface with cornstarch to prevent sticking. (See A.) Roll the fondant ¼" (6 mm) thick. As you roll, sprinkle the fondant with cornstarch and check underneath to be sure your fondant is not sticking. (See B.) Sprinkle the work surface with additional cornstarch as necessary.

2. Cut out a fondant circle with the round cutter. Your cutter should be the same size as the top of your cupcakes. (See C.) Brush off excess cornstarch with a dry brush.

3. Using the offset spatula, spread a thin layer of smooth buttercream on a cupcake. (See D.)

4. Place the fondant circle on the cupcake and smooth it across the top and around the edges. (See E.)

Tips

- Powdered sugar is a good alternative for cornstarch. However, cornstarch is best because it is drier—and does not contain sugar which can make your fondant sticky.

- If your cupcake has a dome top, trim the top before icing.

- Fill a mesh tea-ball infuser with cornstarch for easy dusting. (See A.)

- Use a dry pastry brush to remove cornstarch from fondant. To give the fondant a shiny appearance, brush with a clear alcohol, such as vodka. For a slight shimmer, add a small amount of luster dust to the vodka.

Silicone Molds

- fondant-covered cupcakes (blue shown)
- cornstarch
- colored fondant (pink, green and brown shown)
- silicone mold (cherry blossom or design of your choice)
- small paintbrush

Silicone molds are used to make detailed fondant and gum paste decorations. They can also be used for chocolate, candy, clay, ice, butter, and many other applications. They are soft and flexible, and can go from oven to freezer without affecting the mold. However, they are expensive, so before purchasing a silicone mold make sure it is something you will use again.

Tip:

To save time you can make some of your mold shapes in advance. However, once they dry they will not bend or curve to the shape of the cupcake.

Let's Go!

(A) *dust mold with cornstarch*

(B) *press into mold*

1. Dust the mold with cornstarch to prevent sticking. (See A.)

2. Pinch off a piece of fondant about the size of the mold. Press the fondant into the mold. (See B.)

3. Bend the mold to release the fondant shape. (See C.)

4. Lightly brush the backside of the fondant shape with water to remove any cornstarch and make the piece sticky. (See D.)

5. Place the fondant shape on the cupcake. (See E.)

(C) *bend mold to release*

(D) *brush backside with water*

(E) *place on cupcake*

You'll Need

- cupcakes
- colorful fondant (green shown)
- cornstarch
- cupcake with thin layer of buttercream (see recipe on page 133)
- small fondant rolling pin
- impression mat
- 2¼" (5.5 cm) round cookie cutter
- small paintbrush

Tip

- Fondant circles can be made ahead, dried, and used as toppers on frosted cupcakes.

- Plastic molds are more affordable and often have more variety in shapes and sizes. The plastic molds are not flexible like silicone, so they are a little harder to release the fondant, but they work well for simple shapes.

Impression mats add texture and a specific design to your fondant. They are often used for cake decorating but are also great for cupcake toppers. The mats are typically not as detailed as silicone molds, but they are more affordable because they are made of plastic.

Let's Go!

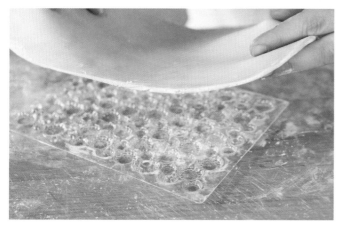

(A) *place fondant over mat*

(B) *press fondant with fingers to get the most detail*

(C) *cut out disk*

(D) *place on cupcake and smooth*

1. Roll the fondant ¼" (6 mm) thick. See Lab 11 (page 34) for how to roll out fondant.

2. Place the fondant over the impression mat. (See A.)

3. Roll with the rolling pin or press the fondant into the mat with your fingers. (See B.) Remove the mat.

4. Cut out a fondant circle with the round cutter. (See C.) Brush off excess cornstarch with a dry brush.

5. Place the fondant circle on a cupcake and smooth it across the top and around the edges. Decorate with fondant buttons if desired. (See D.)

- frosted cupcakes
- colored fondant (gray shown)
- cornstarch
- gel food coloring (black and red shown)
- fondant rolling pin
- rubber stamps (Eiffel Tower and heart or design of your choice)
- small paintbrush
- 2" (5 cm) round cookie cutter

Stamping is a quick and simple way to get a detailed design onto your cupcake. There are many types of stamps available at your local craft store, or purchase a custom-made stamp with your monogram or other design for a wedding or shower.

Tips

- Make sure the size of your rubber stamp is smaller than the circle cutter.
- Fondant disks can be made in advance. Let them dry for a few hours on a sheet tray, and then store them in an airtight container at room temperature with parchment or wax paper between layers.
- The fondant rounds can be cut out prior to stamping. However, we found it easier to stamp the large piece of fondant and cut disks after stamping.

Let's Go!

(A) *paint stamp with food coloring*

(B) *stamp on fondant*

(C) *cut out disk*

(D) *stamp again*

1. Roll out the fondant ¼" (6 mm) thick. See Lab 11 (page 34) for details on rolling out fondant.
2. Paint the larger stamp evenly with food coloring. (See A.) Stamp on the fondant, leaving space between the designs to cut out rounds for other cupcakes. (See B.) Re-apply food coloring to the stamp as needed.
3. Use the round cutter to cut out fondant disks. (See C.) Stamp with additional designs to fill in the white space if you desire. (See D.) Let fondant disks dry for a few hours.
4. Place the disks on top of the frosted cupcakes.

Taking it Further

To make a repetitive pattern that bleeds off the topper edges, simply stamp a pattern across the entire piece of rolled out fondant. Proceed with step 3.

Stenciling on fondant

- frosted cupcakes
- fondant
- cornstarch
- royal icing (see recipe on page 136; soft peak consistency; white shown or color of your choice)
- white sanding sugar
- fondant roller
- stencil (snowflake and swirly patterns shown, or design of your choice)
- 4" (10 cm) offset spatula
- 2" (5 cm) round cutter

Tips

- You will need to clean your stencil periodically if the icing leaks to the underside.
- These disks can be made in advance. Let them dry for a few hours on a sheet tray. Store in an airtight container at room temperature with parchment or wax paper between the layers.

Stenciling can add an amazing amount of detail to your cupcake toppers with very little effort. It takes some practice, but it is a lot quicker than piping all the detail. After removing the stencil you can leave the icing as is or sprinkle the design with sanding sugar while the icing is still wet.

Let's Go!

(A) *spread icing across stencil*

(B) *remove excess icing*

(C) *remove the stencil*

(D) *cut out disks*

(E) *sprinkle with sugar*

1. Roll out the fondant ¼" (6 mm) thick. See Lab 11 (page 34) for details on rolling out fondant.

2. Place the stencil flat on top of the fondant. Hold one end of the stencil in place, and spread a thin layer of the royal icing across the stencil with your spatula. (See A.) Remove any excess icing with the spatula so there is an even, thin layer. (See B.) Peel the stencil off the fondant. (See C.)

3. Use the round cutter to cut out fondant disks. (See D.) Be careful not to smudge your design when moving the disks. If desired, sprinkle the disk with sanding sugar before the icing dries. (See E.) Let the fondant disks dry for a few hours.

4. Place the disks on top of the cupcakes.

Royal Icing

ROYAL ICING IS A SMOOTH WHITE ICING consisting of egg whites and powdered sugar that colors nicely. Royal icing can be thickened and piped into very fine details, or thinned out and used to fill in outlines. Either way, it dries hard when left at room temperature. In this unit, we will learn a few piping techniques, how to make ornate filigree toppers, and how to decorate sugar cookies.

UNIT 4

Piping on fondant

- cupcakes covered in fondant
- royal icing (see recipe on page 136; medium-peak consistency) in a 12" (30 cm) pastry bag fitted with #2 round tip
- clear alcohol (such as vodka)
- edible luster dust (silver shown)
- edible dragees (silver shown)
- small paintbrush

Royal icing is perfect for piping intricate designs on fondant. Buttercream is not the best choice because it often has air bubbles and will not look as pristine. A popular wedding cake design is swirled piping often called scrollwork, as on the cupcake shown. It takes a little practice but it is a very elegant pattern.

Tips

- If you make a mistake, wipe the royal icing off with an offset spatula or toothpick. If some icing remains, use a damp paintbrush to remove it.
- Draw or trace a design on parchment paper. Practice piping on top of the design.

Let's Go!

(A) *pipe large swirl in center*

(B) *pipe smaller swirls*

(C) *pipe dot and drag tip through*

1. To pipe with royal icing, hold the piping bag at a slight angle about ⅛" (3 mm) from the cupcake surface. Apply gentle and even pressure to the bag while moving it in the desired pattern. Release the pressure right before the stopping point, and pull the tip away.

2. For this design, start with one spiral in the center. (See A.) Continue to pipe five large spirals around the cupcake.

3. Pipe smaller swirls off of each large spiral. (See B.) To make the smallest swirls, pipe a dot close to a swirl and drag the pastry tip through the dot to connect it to the existing swirl. (See C.)

4. Allow the icing to dry completely. Mix the luster dust with some clear alcohol. Carefully paint the scrollwork. (See D.) Pipe additional small dots and add silver dragees, if desired.

(D) *paint the scrollwork*

Brush Embroidery

- cupcakes covered in fondant (turquoise shown)
- colored royal icing (see recipe on page 136; medium/stiff peak consistency; pink, yellow, purple shown)
- water
- 12 " (30 cm) pastry bag fitted with #2 round tip
- small paintbrush

Brush embroidery is a classic cake-decorating technique. It is typically floral in design and has the appearance of lace. Traditionally found on white wedding cakes, these bright cupcakes are a nice surprise.

Tip

If you find it difficult to pipe freehand, use a flower cookie cutter or stamp as a guide. While the fondant is still soft, lightly press the cutter or stamp into the fondant to make an impression.

Let's Go!

(A) *pipe outline of flower*

(B) *brush lines of icing toward center*

(C) *pipe smaller flower*

(D) *add dots to center*

1. Using the royal icing, pipe the outline of a large flower on the fondant. (See A.)

2. Dip the paintbrush into the water and remove excess to make it damp. While the icing is still wet, brush the lines of icing toward the center of the flower with the damp brush. Use quick, short strokes and clean the brush as needed. (See B.)

3. Pipe a smaller flower inside the larger flower and repeat the brush technique. (See C.) Add small dots to the flower center. (See D.)

- cupcakes
- royal icing (see recipe on page 136; medium/stiff peak consistency) in 12" (30 cm) pastry bag with round tip #3
- template
- parchment paper or acetate sheet (if using acetate, rub with a little shortening)
- 4" (10 cm) offset spatula
- silver dragees (optional)

In this lab you will learn to make royal icing toppers, specifically filigree crowns. These embellishments have to be made in advance because they need to dry for a few days. Royal icing decorations are very fragile so be sure to make extra. You can use this same technique to make a solid shape called a run-out, which we address in the tips. I like to use this method for making letters or numbers because you can print out a specific font for a template and trace it.

Tips

- Draw your own templates or trace around cookie cutters directly onto the parchment paper. Flip the paper over before outlining with icing so the ink does not dry into the decoration. Outline the shape with royal icing.

- For run-outs, outline your design with thicker royal icing. Flood the inside with runny royal icing. Proceed with step 4.

Let's Go!

1. Place your template underneath the parchment paper or acetate. (See A.) Outline your image with icing. (See B.)

2. Fill in the design with random swirls of piping. (See C.) The closer the piping, the more stable the decoration will be. If you are adding more than one color, let the icing dry a few hours between applications so the colors do not bleed.

4. Let the decorations dry at least 24 hours. It is best to make these a few days ahead of time to ensure they are completely dry. Drying time will depend on humidity and size of the decoration. (See D.)

5. Once dry, gently slide the offset spatula under the royal icing decoration to separate it from the paper. Alternatively, you can put the design near the edge of the table and peel the paper away. (See E.) Place on cupcake. Add silver dragees or embellishments if desired.

(A) *place acetate over template*

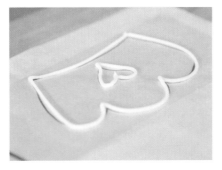

(B) *outline your image*

(C) *fill in with swirls*

(D) *let dry*

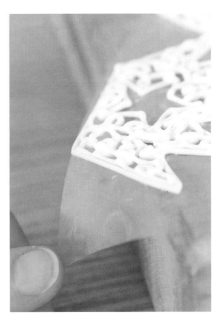

(E) *peel the decoration away from acetate*

Sugar Cookie Toppers

- frosted cupcakes
- baked sugar cookies 1"–3" (2.5–7.5 cm) in size (see recipe on page 142; dog theme or design of your choice)
- royal icing (see recipe on page 136; medium peak consistency; white, red, black and brown shown) in 12" (30 cm) pastry bags with #3 round tips
- royal icing (see recipe on page 136) in bowls (runny consistency)
- sanding sugar if desired
- 4" (10 cm) offset spatula

One of my favorite things to do is to decorate sugar cookies. We have hundreds of cutters at the bakery and we are always trying new shapes and designs. Children and adults love them because they look great and taste delicious. In this lab you'll learn some tricks for decorating sugar cookies, and then we will show you how to use them as toppers for your cupcakes. We chose a dog theme, but you can use these techniques with any sugar cookie shape.

Tip

Letting the iced cookies dry at least 6–8 hours is very important before adding another color. If you add another color too soon, the colors will bleed over time. Humidity can affect the drying time too; it is best to keep cookies in a cool, dry place. Do not refrigerate or the icing will get soft and tacky.

Let's Go!

1. Using a pastry bag, outline the cookie with the icing as close to the edge as you can. (See A and B.)

2. Using the runny royal icing and small offset spatula, fill in the outline. (See C.) Be sure to add enough icing to fill the cookie evenly, but not so much that it will run over the edge. Let cookies dry at least 6–8 hours before adding another color. I recommend drying overnight for bright colors.

3. To add spots, add dots of a different-colored icing immediately after filling in the outline. The spots will settle into the runny icing.

4. Pipe details onto cookies with the royal icing pastry bag. To add decorative accents such as sugar or other details, pipe in the area where you want the accents to stick. (See D.) Dip the cookie into bowl of sanding sugar. (See E.) Add eyes or other accents. (See F.) Repeat with the remaining cookies. Let dry.

5. Center each cookie on top of the frosted cupcake.

(A) *outline with royal icing*

(B) *outline close to edge*

(C) *fill in the outline*

(D) *pipe icing where you want sugar*

(E) *dip in sugar*

(F) *add accents*

Flowers & Garden

IN OUR BAKERY, flowers are the most requested design, whether it's for a cake, cookie, or a cupcake. We are constantly creating new designs and combinations to keep things fun and fresh. In this unit you will learn some of the basics but with a contemporary twist, therefore I am not including the classic buttercream rose.

UNIT 5

Buttercream Flower

- cupcakes
- colored buttercream (see recipe on page 133; orange shown) in 12" (30 cm) pastry bag fitted with large C-shaped ruffle tip, such as Wilton #402
- colored buttercream (see recipe on page 133; pink shown) in 12" (30 cm) pastry bag fitted with small C-shaped ruffle tip, such as Wilton tip #401 or #79, or Ateco #81
- colored buttercream (see recipe on page 133; lime green shown) in 12" (30 cm) pastry bag with large grass tip, such as Ateco #234 or small #3 round tip

A big, bold buttercream flower on top of a cupcake makes a statement. In this lab, you will learn to pipe a flower directly onto the cupcake in two different sizes. This particular flower is fast and forgiving if your technique is not perfect. You do not have to use a flower nail as when making roses—perfect for beginners!

Tip

Keeping the buttercream on the top of the cupcakes and away from the sides will help prevent them from sticking together in a box.

Let's Go!

(A) pipe around cupcake pulling up and out

(B) pipe inside outer circle

(D) use grass tip for center

1. Using the larger C-shaped tip, pipe around the edge of the cupcake, pulling up and out at a slight angle. Release pressure and pull away from the cupcake. (See A.)

2. Continue to pipe inside the outer circle making petals slightly smaller as you move in toward the center. (See B and C.)

3. Use the grass tip to add a center to the flower. (See D.)

4. Alternatively, you can use the smaller C-shaped tip for the entire flower. Use the same method, but add more petals. For the center of this flower, use the small round tip to create a cluster of dots. (See E.)

(C) pipe smaller petals as you move toward center

(E) make dots for center

Buttercream Rosettes

- cupcakes
- colored buttercream (see recipe on page 133; bright pink shown) in 14"–18" (36–46 cm) pastry bag with large open star tip, such as Wilton tip #1M or #2D
- colored buttercream (see recipe on page 133; bright pink shown) in 14"–18" (36–46 cm) pastry bag with small open star tip, such as Ateco tip #21 or #30

Rosettes are a classic piping technique, and are more traditionally used for borders on cakes. It is now common to see entire cakes covered in buttercream rosettes for a young girl's birthday party or a wedding dessert table. Vary the pastry tip size for a larger or smaller pattern on these cupcakes.

Tip

Rosettes look pretty as a border on a cake or cupcake. Use a very small star tip for cupcake borders.

Let's Go!

(A) *using large tip, pipe rosettes around the edge*

(B) *continue to pipe toward center*

(D) *continue inside toward center*

1. Practice making a rosette on a piece of parchment paper. Hold the bag vertically at a ninety-degree angle to the paper, with the tip about ¼" (6 mm) from the surface. Apply pressure to the bag and make a small star. Continue with even pressure, and make a tight circle around the star. Release the pressure and pull the tip away. When you feel comfortable, decorate the cupcakes.

2. Using the larger tip, pipe around the edge of a cupcake making five or six rosettes. (See A.) Pipe one rosette in the center. (See B.)

3. Alternatively, using the smaller tip, pipe around the edge making ten to twelve rosettes. (See C.) Continue inside outer circle, making four or five more rosettes. (See D.) Add one to the center. (See E.)

(C) *using small tip, pipe rosettes around edge*

(E) *finish in center*

Fondant Rose Bouquet

- cupcakes covered in fondant (white shown)
- colored fondant (yellow shown)
- cornstarch
- water
- small fondant roller
- wheel pastry cutter or pizza cutter
- small paint brush

Rolled roses or ribbon roses are quick and fun to make. They have a more contemporary look than traditional fondant roses. We make plenty of the conventional buttercream and fondant roses at our bakery, but they require each petal to be made individually, which is time consuming when making multiple cupcakes. This method is not only quicker, but it can be done in advance, too.

Tips

- For larger roses, cut the fondant strips wider.
- For leaves, roll out fondant ⅛" (3 mm) thick; cut into squares. Brush a little water in the center of each square. Fold two opposite corners together and pinch. Cut across the center of the pinched fondant to create two leaves from each square.

Let's Go!

(A) cut strips and roll one at a time

(B) pinch to open up rose

(C) cut off excess fondant

1. Roll out fondant ⅛" (3 mm) thick. See Lab 11 (page 34) for details on rolling out fondant. Cut 1" (2.5 cm)-wide strips with a wheel cutter, using a ruler as a guide, if desired.

2. Start rolling up one strip at a time. (See A.) Pinch the bottom as you go to open up the rose. (See B.) I like to pinch the top as I roll the fondant to thin the rose edges to make it look more realistic. Continue rolling until you reach the desired size rose; cut off the excess fondant and use it for another rose. (See C.) If your rose is not sticking together, brush a little water on the end to seal the fondant. Pull the edges back with your fingers to open up the rose.

3. Brush a little water on the bottom of the rose and place on the cupcake. (See D.)

(D) place on cupcake

- frosted cupcakes
- colored gum paste
- cornstarch
- luster or petal dust
- royal icing (see recipe on page 136) in 12" (30 cm) pastry bag with #3 round tip
- small fondant roller
- 1"–3" (2.5–7.5 cm) flower cutters
- foam pad
- ball tool
- toothpicks or a veiner (hydrangea and leaf veiner shown)
- egg carton or aluminum foil
- paintbrush

In this lab, you will learn how to make push flowers, which are small and relatively quick to create. The blossoms require some drying time, but can be made months ahead. They are brought to life with a brush of luster dust or petal dust, which gives them dimension and a realistic appearance.

Tips

- Fondant can be used instead of gum paste, but the flowers will take longer to dry.
- Luster dust has a shimmer and adds a little sparkle. Petal dust is dry coloring and gives a matte finish. Focus on shading the centers and edges of the flowers to give them a realistic look.

Let's Go!

1. Knead the gum paste until pliable. Roll out the gum paste ⅛" (3 mm) thick using cornstarch as needed to prevent sticking. Cut out flowers with the flower cutter, then cover with plastic wrap until ready to use.

2. Place a flower on the foam pad and thin the edges by rolling over them with the ball tool. (See A.)

3. Use a toothpick to add grooves in your petals. (See B.)

4. Alternatively, press the flower into a veiner. (See C.)

5. Leaf veiners are wonderful for adding realistic impressions to your flower leaves. (See D.)

6. Let the flowers and leaves dry in egg cartons or over crumpled aluminum foil to add dimension and curves. Add centers, if desired with royal icing or dragees.

7. Brush with luster or petal dust. (See E.) Place on frosted cupcakes.

(A) roll over edges with ball tool

(D) leaf veiner

(B) toothpick adds dimension

(C) or place in veiner

(E) brush with dust

Sugar Flowers

- frosted cupcakes
- gum paste or fondant (purple shown)
- cornstarch
- small fondant roller
- 1¼" (3 cm) round cutter
- 1½" (4 cm) fluted round cutter
- foam pad
- plastic wrap
- ball tool
- edible glue (such as tylose powder mixed with water) or egg white
- egg carton
- paintbrush

In this lab, you will learn how to make a ruffly sugar flower with three layers. This is a great layered flower for beginners because it requires few tools and is easier to put together than a sugar flower consisting of individual petals. This technique can be used to make larger flowers for wedding cakes by adding more layers.

Tip

To make a very simple carnation-style ruffled flower, make 2–3 flower- or round-shaped cutouts and layer them together to create ruffles. Then continue with step 5.

Let's Go!

1. Knead the gum paste until pliable. Roll a piece of gum paste or fondant into a 1" (2.5 cm) ball. Roll the ball between your hands to form a cone shape. Using your fingers, create a hole in top of the cone, and then thin out edges all around to create a ruffly center for your flower. Pinch off excess gum paste and let dry. (See A.)

2. Roll out additional gum paste or fondant ⅛" (3 mm) thick, using cornstarch as needed. Cut out flower layers with the two cutters. (See B.)

3. Place the flower-shaped cut-outs one at a time on the foam pad. Cover the remaining fondant pieces with plastic wrap so they do not dry out. Thin and curl the petal edges by rolling over them with the ball tool. (See C.) Continue with round cut outs. (See D.) While working on the other petals, let the layers dry in an egg carton to give them a curved shape.

4. Layer the petals around the center, pinching them together to create ruffles. Use glue or egg white to secure the layers together.

5. Let the flowers dry a few hours or overnight in an egg carton to retain the shape. (See E.)

6. Brush the flowers with luster or petal dust. Place on frosted cupcakes.

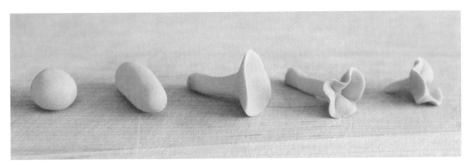

(A) steps for the centers

(B) cutting out flower shape

(D) cut additional layers and thin edges

(C) thin and roll over edge with ball tool

(E) let dry in egg carton

Butterflies in the Grass

- cupcakes
- wafer paper printed with edible image (butterflies shown or design of your choice)
- luster dust (silver shown)
- edible clear gel (piping gel)
- sanding sugar (white shown)
- green buttercream (see recipe on page 133) in a pastry bag with grass tip #234 Wilton or Ateco
- small craft scissors
- small paintbrush
- egg carton

Edible wafer paper is made from potato starch and is printed with USDA-approved food coloring. We bought the butterfly images online, where there are a large variety of prints and patterns available. You can also print your own images if you have an edible-image printer (more common among professionals).

Tip

These water paper butterflies will keep for months if stored in an airtight container.

Let's Go!

(A) cut out the images

(B) paint a thin layer of gel

(C) sprinkle with sugar

(D) let dry in egg carton

1. Carefully cut out the butterflies with the scissors; wafer paper is fragile. (See A.)

2. Stir luster dust into the edible clear gel for a sparkly effect, if desired. Paint a thin layer of gel onto each butterfly. (See B.)

3. Sprinkle with sanding sugar. (See C.)

4. Fold the butterfly down the center so the wings stick up; let dry in egg carton to hold its shape. (See D.)

5. Pipe green grass onto the cupcakes. Place butterflies on cupcakes, along with sugar flowers or other nature-inspired decorations.

26 Herb Pots

- chocolate cupcakes
- buttercream (see recipe on page 133) in a pastry bag fitted with a large round tip, such as Ateco #806
- fresh herbs
- 3" (7.5 cm) terra-cotta pot

Herb pots make adorable centerpieces and favors, and they are even better when they are edible. These cupcake pots are easy and versatile—top them with sugar veggies, edible flowers, or lollipop flowers. This is a fun project for a birthday party too.

Take It Further

- Sculpt vegetables out of fondant or gum paste to decorate the top.
- Write names on craft sticks and stick one in each pot. Use as a place setting at a garden shower or outdoor wedding.

Let's Go!

(A) *cut off cupcake top*

(B) *crumble cupcake top into pot*

(D) *cover with cupcake crumbs*

1. Cut off the top of the cupcake. (See A.)
2. Crumble the cupcake top into the bottom of the pot. (See B.)
3. Pipe a small amount of buttercream into the pot.
4. Place a cupcake in the pot. Cover the cupcake with buttercream. (See C.)
5. Sprinkle with additional cupcake crumbs. You will need about one-half of an extra cupcake to crumble per pot. (See D.)
6. Place herbs in the pot. (See E.)

(C) *cover cupcake with buttercream*

(E) *add herbs*

Fun Themes

BOTH KIDS AND ADULTS WILL ENJOY the creative and festive ideas presented here for your next party. We will incorporate some techniques we have already learned, like working with fondant in "Gone Surfing." We will make drink-inspired cupcakes, which are always a hit at cocktail parties and showers, especially the fresh mint mojitos. And we will even learn to make a huge cupcake cake!

UNIT

6

Krispie S'more Cupcakes

- Rice Krispie Treat mixture, still warm
- nonstick spray
- ganache (see recipe on page 135) in a 14" (36 cm) pastry bag fitted with a star tip, such as Ateco #826
- graham cracker crumbs
- sanding sugar
- standard size cupcake pan
- ice-cream scoop
- 4" (10 cm) offset spatula

Rice Krispie Treats and s'mores are favorite childhood treats. We combined both of these into one cupcake. There is no baking required and you can make them gluten free with Gluten Free Rice Krispies.

Tip

If you prefer less chocolate and more marshmallow, you can pipe a thin layer of ganache on top of the cupcake and top it with a marshmallow meringue frosting.

Let's Go!

(A) *scoop treats into pan*

(B) *press into pan*

(D) *pipe ganache on top*

1. Spray a standard size cupcake pan with nonstick spray. Scoop the warm Rice Krispie Treats into the pan using an ice cream scoop. (See A.) Press the mixture into the pan. (See B.) Sprinkle some graham cracker crumbs on top. Let it set about 30 minutes until cool.

2. Remove the Krispie cupcakes with an offset spatula and dip the edges in graham cracker crumbs. (See C.)

3. Pipe ganache in a swirl on top. (See D.)

4. Sprinkle with graham cracker crumbs and sanding sugar. (See E.)

(C) *edge with graham crumbs*

(E) *add graham cracker crumbs and sugar*

Doughnut Cupcakes

- frosted cupcakes
- vanilla cupcake batter (see recipe on page 140) in pastry bag fitted with large round tip, such as Ateco #804
- colored royal icing (see recipe on page 136; medium peak consistency; pink, blue, green shown)
- multicolored sprinkles or nonpareils
- nonstick mini-doughnut mold
- 4" (10 cm) offset spatula

Colorful doughnuts with sprinkles make us all feel like kids again. These cupcakes are perfect for a brunch or child's party. For ease of the recipe we made doughnuts with the cupcake batter, but this would also be delicious with a classic cake-doughnut recipe.

Tip

For chocolate dipped doughnuts, simply dip tops in warm ganache.

Let's Go!

(A) *pipe batter into mold*

(B) *ice the doughnuts*

(C) *add sprinkles*

(D) *place on cupcake*

1. Pipe batter into the mini-doughnut mold. (See A.) Bake in 350°F (180°C, or gas mark 4) oven until the toothpick tests clean, about 10–12 minutes; let cool 3–5 minutes. Turn the doughnuts out of the pan onto a sheet tray; cool completely.

2. Spread icing on top of the doughnut using the spatula. (See B.)

3. Add colorful sprinkles over the icing. (See C.) Let the doughnuts set 5–10 minutes.

4. Place a doughnut on top of an iced cupcake. (See D.)

- cupcakes
- tropical colors of fondant (orange, red, yellow, blue shown)
- cornstarch
- water
- ocean-blue buttercream (see recipe on page 133)
- graham cracker crumbs
- sanding sugar
- small fondant roller
- 1" (2.5 cm) flower cutter
- paintbrush
- surfboard cookie cutter
- 4" (10 cm) offset spatula
- tropical sugar flowers, sugar starfish and shells (optional)

Beach-themed cupcakes are always fun in the summer! In this lab you will make fondant surfboards that can be made in advance along with other ocean decor you want to include, such as shells and starfish. This fondant technique can be applied to many different shapes and patterns for other seasons.

Tip

Surfboards can be made in advance. Let them dry for a few hours on a sheet tray. Store in an airtight container at room temperature with parchment or wax paper in between layers.

Let's Go!

1. Roll out all the fondant colors ¼" (6 mm) thick using cornstarch as needed to prevent sticking. See Lab 11 (page 34) for details on rolling out fondant. Cut out flowers from three of the colors. (See A.)

2. Place the flowers on top of the fourth color of fondant and roll over until the flowers blend into the lower layer. (See B.) If the flowers are not sticking, add a little water with a paintbrush on the back side of the flower.

3. Cut out surfboards with the surfboard cutter; let dry at least one hour. (See C and D.)

4. Using the offset spatula, frost the cupcakes with blue buttercream, swirling to create peaks similar to waves. (See E.)

5. Mix the graham cracker crumbs with sanding sugar. Sprinkle one half of the top of the cupcake with the mixture to create sand. (See F.) Place the surfboards on top. Garnish with tropical sugar flowers, sugar starfish and shells, if desired.

(A) cut out fondant flowers

(D) let dry

(B) roll flowers into fondant

(E) create waves with blue icing

(C) cut out shapes

(F) add sand to cupcake

30 White Chocolate Snowman

- frosted cupcakes with shredded coconut topping
- white chocolate truffle mix, chilled (see recipe on page 140)
- finely shredded coconut
- black royal icing (see recipe on page 136; medium peak consistency) in pastry bag fitted with #3 round tip
- flexible candy strips (Air Heads Extremes Sweetly Sour Belts candy shown)
- small 1¼" (3 cm) ice-cream scoop (#70)
- toothpicks
- sheet tray lined with parchment or wax paper
- small craft scissors

In this lab you'll learn to make white chocolate, coconut truffle snowmen. You can get creative and use a variety of candy to decorate the snowmen. We kept it simple by using one candy and one color of royal icing. A fondant hat would be cute too!

Tip

Looking for a simpler treat? These truffles are wonderful on their own!

Let's Go!

(A) roll truffle mix into balls

(B) roll in coconut

(E) cut candy in half

1. Scoop the truffle mix and roll into round balls. (See A.) Roll in finely shredded coconut and place on the tray. (See B.)

2. Spear one ball with a toothpick. (See C.) Add another ball for the head. (See D.) Chill if snowmen are soft and difficult to handle.

3. For the scarves, use the scissors to cut the candy strips in half lengthwise. (See E.) Trim the length to fit around the snowman's neck, and cut 1" (2.5 cm) slits on the ends for fringe. Attach the scarf to the snowman with royal icing. Cut triangles from the candy for a nose; attach with royal icing. (See F.)

4. Add eyes with black royal icing. Insert the toothpick that is protruding from the snowman into cupcake. (See G.)

(C) spear with toothpick

(F) add scarf and nose

(D) stack two truffles

(G) add snowman to cupcake

Cupcake Cake

- cupcakes
- colored buttercream (see recipe on page 133; brown shown) in 14"–18" (35–46 cm) pastry bags fitted with large basketweave tip, such as Ateco #897
- colored buttercream (see recipe on page 133; brown and green shown) in 14"–18" (35–46 cm) pastry bags fitted with large star tip, such as Wilton #1M or Ateco #826
- fondant decorations (leaves and acorns shown)
- cake board or platter

Tip

If you are arranging the cupcakes in a custom design, draw the shape onto your board, or make a template out of parchment or wax paper.

A cupcake cake is a cake that uses cupcakes as the base and is frosted to look like a large cake. They are also called pull-apart cakes because you separate the cupcakes to serve them. Most cupcake cakes are iced flat to look like a smooth cake. We love the texture in this cake created by frosting the cupcakes with a star tip.

Let's Go!

(A) arrange cupcakes in desired shape

(C) frost and decorate

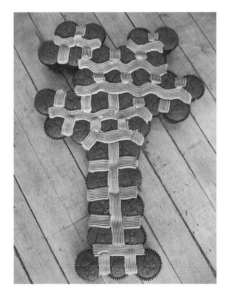

(B) cross hatch with buttercream

1. Arrange the cupcakes in the desired shape on a cake board or platter. (See A.)

2. If you are transporting the cake or moving it around, spread a little royal icing or buttercream underneath most of the cupcakes to secure them to the board. When arranging the cupcakes, push them together to avoid large gaps.

3. Using the large basket weave tip, pipe buttercream in between the cupcakes, creating a crosshatch design. (See B.) Chill the cupcakes, if possible, to set the buttercream.

4. Continue to frost and decorate as desired, using the brown buttercream for the trunk and branches, and the green for the leaves. (See C.) You can be creative and design your own tree.

(D) add fondant decorations

5. Add fondant or sugar decorations as desired. (See D.)

- mini cupcakes
- ganache (see recipe on page 135; may need extra heavy cream to thin ganache as needed.)
- sweet icing fondue (see recipe below)
- cut up fruit: strawberries, pineapple, bananas, oranges
- toppings: colorful sprinkles, chopped nuts, coconut, candy pieces, chocolate chips
- fondue pot (for chocolate fondue)
- fondue or bamboo skewers

Dessert fondue is a wonderful communal activity for a dinner party or child's birthday. In this lab you will make chocolate fondue and sweet icing fondue. Mini cupcakes and fruit are dipped and then decorated with sprinkles and delightful toppings. Be sure to have plates and napkins handy because this can get messy, but it's lots of fun.

Sweet Icing Fondue

To make sweet icing fondue, whisk together 3 cups (375 g) powdered sugar, ⅓ cup (80 ml) milk, and a splash of vanilla extract or squirt of lemon juice. To make a fruit-flavored icing, substitute fruit juice for the milk. If the icing is too thick, thin with additional milk or juice.

Let's Go!

(A) *make ganache thin enough to dip*

(B) *dip cupcake into fondue*

(C) *decorate with toppings*

1. For chocolate fondue, make ganache and use it while still warm, or place over a double boiler to rewarm. Thin the ganache with heavy cream as needed to reach dipping consistency. If the ganache is too thick your cupcakes may fall apart in the fondue. (See A.)

2. Sweet icing fondue does not need to be heated. Thin with additional liquid as needed.

3. Instruct your guests to skewer a cupcake and dip it into the icing or fondue. (See B.) It is best not to submerge the entire cupcake, because you may lose it in the fondue.

4. Decorate the cupcakes with cut up fruit and other toppings as desired. (See C.)

Tip

Add a splash of liqueur to the ganache, such as coffee, hazelnut, or orange.

Espresso Cups

- chocolate cupcakes (see recipe on page 136) baked in oven-safe espresso cups
- mocha buttercream (see recipe below)
- vanilla buttercream (see recipe on page 133)
- 2 food-safe squeeze bottles
- toothpicks

I love coffee and, of course, any dessert that incorporates chocolate and espresso. These cups are a nice dessert for a romantic Italian dinner. Because they are made in espresso cups, they are a bit smaller and less indulgent. Add a scoop of gelato or biscotti on the side for a more substantial dessert. In this lab you will learn a new technique of melting buttercream and using it as a topping.

Tip

To make mocha buttercream, mix a small amount of instant espresso powder with hot water to create a wet paste. Add the paste to chocolate buttercream to taste.

Let's Go!

(A) *trim cupcakes so they sit below the top of the espresso cups*

(B) *cover with mocha buttercream*

(D) *use toothpick to create heart design*

1. The cupcakes should sit below the top of the espresso cups; trim the cupcakes if they dome above the cup. (See A.)

2. Melt mocha and vanilla buttercream separately in double boiler or microwave. Place each buttercream in a squeeze bottle.

3. Fill the espresso cups with the mocha buttercream to cover the cupcakes. (See B.)

4. Using the vanilla buttercream, add single or multiple dots on each cupcake. (See C.) Draw a toothpick through the dots to form hearts, or connect the dots to create unique patterns. (See D & E.) Have fun with it and create your own designs.

(C) *add dots with vanilla buttercream*

(E) *more designs*

Tea Party

- cupcakes
- sugar cubes
- colored royal icing (see recipe on page 136; purple and green shown) in pastry bags fitted with round tip #2; small leaf tip, such as Ateco #349 or Wilton #352; small open star tip, such as Wilton #16
- sanding sugar
- buttercream (see recipe on page 133) in pastry bag fitted with large round tip, such as Ateco #806
- honey
- teacup

Tip

Make a spicy chai cupcake batter by adding a pinch each of cinnamon, cloves, cardamom, ginger, and black pepper to your vanilla cupcake batter prior to baking.

Specialty teas, like coffee, are gaining popularity across the world and are often used in desserts. In this lab you will learn to decorate sugar cubes, which make a cute gift at a tea-inspired shower or luncheon. I love the idea of serving these cupcakes in mismatched vintage teacups.

Let's Go!

(A) *add green leaf to hydrangea*

(B) *swirly piping*

(D) *drizzle with honey*

1. Piping on sugar cubes can take some practice because they are so small. Simple flowers or monograms are sweet. For a hydrangea, pipe very small stars in a circle and mound them in the center to create a round flower. Add a green leaf at the edge. (See A.)

2. Swirling piping is quick and fun. (See B.)

3. For colorful sugar cubes, coat one side in colorful icing, and then dip it in sanding sugar. (See C.)

4. Place a cupcake in a teacup. Pipe buttercream on top of the cupcake, and drizzle with honey. Serve with the sugar cubes on the side. (See D & E.)

(C) *dip one side in sugar*

(E) *designs*

- vanilla cupcakes (see recipe on page 146)
- lime slices
- white sanding sugar
- lime curd (see recipe on page 142)
- fresh mint buttercream (see recipe below) in a pastry bag with large round tip, such as Ateco #806
- fresh mint sprigs
- rocks glasses

A mojito is a traditional Cuban drink consisting of rum, mint, sugar, lime, and sparkling water. It is a popular refreshing drink, and the flavors are irresistible. In this lab, you'll learn how to make a virgin mojito cupcake, but you can brush the cake layers with rum syrup for a true mojito experience.

Tip

To make fresh mint buttercream, finely chop some fresh mint, and then stir it into the vanilla buttercream (see recipe on page 133).

Let's Go!

(A) *rim glass with lime*

(B) *dip in sanding sugar*

(D) *add a cupcake*

1. Rim the glass with lime, and then dip the glass in sanding sugar to edge the glass. (See A and B.)
2. Fill the bottom of the glass with about 2 tablespoons (30 ml) lime curd. (See C.)
3. Place a cupcake in the glass. (See D.)
4. Frost the cupcake with the mint buttercream. (See E.)
5. Garnish with a mint sprig and lime slice.

(C) *add lime curd*

(E) *frost with mint buttercream*

Taking It Further

For a rum mojito cupcake, brush the cupcake with rum syrup (equal parts simple syrup and rum) before frosting.

Kids
& Babies

IMAGINATIVE, FABULOUS, AND OVER THE TOP,
are terms I'd use to describe many of the baby showers and kid's
parties I've seen lately. So much of the planning is just about
coordination and theme. DIY party decor, favors, and food make
for a fabulous party. These cupcakes are all adorable and relatively
simple. They are sure to make your party a hit!

UNIT 7

Tutu Cupcakes

- cupcakes
- colored fondant (pink shown)
- royal icing (see recipe on page 136; stiff peak consistency) in pastry bag fitted with #3 round tip
- edible pearls
- edible luster dust (optional; pink shown)
- colored buttercream in 14"–18" (35–46 cm) pastry bag fitted with ruffle tip, such as Ateco #070
- fondant rolling pin
- sleeveless dress cookie cutter
- paring knife

The tutu cupcake is one of our most requested specialty cupcakes at our bakery. They are fun and perfect for a girl's birthday party. Let your little princess choose the colors and design of the bodice, which can be easily altered.

Tip

If the buttercream is soft, it is best to chill the cupcakes before adding the bodice. Once cold, cut a slit in center of the frosting with a paring knife, and insert the bodice into the frosting. For more stability, push the bodice into the cake about ½" (1.3 cm).

Let's Go!

1. Roll the fondant ¼" (6 mm) thick; see Lab 11 (page 34) for how to roll out fondant. Cut out dress shapes using the cookie cutter. (See A.)

2. Cut off the lower portion, leaving only the bodice. Let the bodices dry overnight. (See B.)

3. Using the pastry bag fitted with the ruffle tip, create the tutu on the cupcake. Hold the tip close to the cupcake, apply pressure to release the buttercream, and rotate the cupcake with your other hand to create ruffles. Rotate continuously to create 3–4 rows of ruffles. Sprinkle with sugar pearls, if desired. (See C and D.)

4. Decorate the bodice with beads of royal icing and sugar pearls. Brush with luster dust, if desired. (See E.)

5. Push the lower edge of the bodice into the center of the cupcake. (See F.)

(A) cut out dress shape

(B) cut off bottom of dress to create bodice

(C) pipe ruffles for tutu

(D) pipe second layer of ruffles

(E) decorate the bodice

(F) place bodice in center of ruffles

Ice-Cream-Cone Clowns

- cupcakes with paper liners removed
- 5" (13 cm) iced flower-shaped sugar cookies
- vanilla buttercream in a small bowl
- yellow buttercream (see recipe on page 133) in a 12"–14" (30–36 cm) pastry bag fitted with a small open star tip, such as Wilton or Ateco #18
- orange buttercream (see recipe on page 133) in a 12"–14" (30–36 cm) pastry bag fitted with a large grass tip, such as Ateco #234
- candy coated chocolates, such as M&M's (red and brown shown)
- red licorice rope
- sugar cone
- 4" (10 cm) offset spatula
- scissors

My favorite birthday treat as a child was an ice-cream-cone clown. These cupcake clowns were inspired by those and look very similar. Add a scoop of ice cream on the side when serving for the best of both worlds.

Tip

For a special treat add sprinkles to a cone when filling it with ice cream!

Let's Go!

1. Spread a small dollop of buttercream in the center of a sugar cookie. Place a cupcake upside down on top of the cookie. (See A.)

2. Using the offset spatula, frost the cupcake with a thin layer of vanilla buttercream. (See B.)

3. Pipe a yellow star-tip (such as Ateco #826) border where the cupcake meets the cookie. (See C.)

4. Pipe orange hair on top and all around the cupcake except for the front, which will be the face. (See D.)

5. Place candy pieces on the face for eyes and nose. Use scissors to cut the licorice rope into 2" (5 cm) pieces and position one on the face for the mouth.

6. To add sprinkle trim to the ice cream cones, dip the edges in royal icing, and then dip in colorful sprinkles. (See E.) Do the same for the tip if desired. Let dry on parchment or wax paper. Place the sugar cone on top for the hat.

(A) place cupcake upside down on sugar cookie

(B) frost cupcake

(C) pipe yellow star border

(D) pipe orange hair

(E) dip cones in royal icing and sprinkles

Movie Night Cupcakes

You'll Need

- vanilla cupcakes (red and white striped liner shown)
- vanilla or caramel buttercream (see recipe on page 133) in 14"–18" (36–46 cm) pastry bag fitted with a large round tip, such as Ateco #806
- caramel corn
- caramel sauce
- Sno-Caps
- sea salt

Everyone loves the movies—especially the popcorn and candy. These cupcakes are the ultimate movie night treat. They incorporate sweet and salty caramel corn, Sno-Caps, and cupcakes. Serve these treats at your next awards party or kids' sleepover, and get rave reviews!

Tip

To make caramel buttercream, stir caramel sauce into the vanilla buttercream to taste. Sprinkle with sea salt for salted caramel.

Let's Go!

(A) *frost cupcake*

(C) *drizzle with caramel sauce*

(D) *add Sno-Caps*

(B) *add caramel corn*

1. Frost the cupcakes with a thin layer of vanilla or caramel buttercream. (See A.)

2. Press a handful of caramel corn into the buttercream on top of the cupcakes. (See B.)

3. Drizzle the popcorn with a small amount of the caramel sauce. (See C.) Press Sno-Cap candies into the caramel sauce. (See D.)

4. Sprinkle with sea salt if desired. (See E.)

(E) *sprinkle with sea salt*

Soft Serve Ice Cream

- cupcakes baked in ice cream cones
- vanilla buttercream (see recipe on page 133) in 14"–18" (36–46 cm) pastry bag fitted with a large round tip, such as Ateco #806
- ganache (see recipe on page 135) in bowl at least 4" (10 cm) deep
- sprinkles, such as multicolored nonpareils

What child doesn't love soft serve ice cream dipped in chocolate and loaded with sprinkles? This cupcake treat looks just like those cones, but is filled with cake. For a kid's party activity, let them add their own toppings such as sprinkles, nuts, cherries, and whipped cream.

Tips

- Fill the ice cream cones and stand them in muffin pan. They will be wobbly; carefully put them in the oven. If desired, secure them with aluminum foil in the gaps.
- If the ganache does not set right away, place the cones in the refrigerator to set.

Let's Go!

(A) *frost cupcakes with high swirl*

(C) *drain off excess and let set*

(B) *dip cupcake in ganache*

(D) *roll edge of ganache in sprinkles*

1. Pipe the buttercream on the cupcakes in a swirl motion, about 3" (7.5 cm) high. (See A.)

2. Chill the cupcakes for 20–30 minutes, or until the icing is completely set.

3. Heat some ganache in the microwave or over a double boiler until just warm and fluid.

4. Turn the cupcake upside down and dip into the ganache. (See B.) Let excess ganache drain off for a few seconds. (See C.) Turn the cupcake right side up, and let ganache set about 30 seconds.

5. Roll the edge of the ganache just above the cone in the sprinkles. (See D.)

Owl Cupcakes

- cupcakes
- vanilla buttercream (see recipe on page 133)
- cream-filled chocolate sandwich cookies, such as Oreos
- mini cream-filled chocolate sandwich cookies, such as Mini Oreos
- royal icing (see recipe on page 136)
- mini candy-coated chocolates, such as M&M minis
- jelly beans
- 4" (10 cm) offset spatula

Tip

Let your child design their own cupcakes using these same materials. You'll be surprised how creative they can be with candy making colorful roads, cookie towers, and jelly bean flowers.

My son has loved owls since he started talking. These fluffy, mysterious birds with big eyes make adorable cupcakes. Decorated with candy and cookies, what child wouldn't love them?

Let's Go!

1. Spread a thin layer of buttercream on top of a cupcake. Shingle the mini chocolate candies across the entire cupcake. (See A.)

2. Split open the regular and mini sandwich cookies, and scrape the cream off.

3. Cut the regular size sandwich cookies in half for the wings. Spread a little icing on the back of the wings, and place the wings on the cupcake. (See B and C.)

4. Pipe a dot of royal icing in the center of two mini chocolate cookies, and then add a mini chocolate candy on each for the eyes.

5. Spread a little icing on the back of the eyes and place on the cupcake. (See D.)

6. Add a jelly bean for the owl's beak. (See E.)

(A) *shingle mini chocolate candies on cupcake*

(B) *spread icing on back of wings*

(D) *place eyes on cupcake*

(C) *place on cupcake*

(E) *add jelly bean for beak*

Egg Nests

- cupcakes
- green buttercream (see recipe on page 133) in a 14" (37 cm) pastry bag fitted with a large leaf tip, such as Wilton #366
- brown buttercream (see recipe on page 133) in a 14" (37 cm) pastry bag fitted with a large grass tip, such as Ateco #234
- toasted coconut
- jelly beans

These cute egg nests are perfect for spring parties, baby showers, and Easter celebrations. A lemon cupcake would be delicious with the toasted coconut, or use your favorite cupcake recipe. The jelly beans are a bonus treat for candy lovers.

Tip

Buy speckled jelly beans for a more natural egg look.

Taking it Further

Set the cupcakes inside festive wraps, such as the fences shown.

Let's Go!

(A) add a ring of leaves

(C) pipe more to build up nest

(D) fill nest with coconut

(B) pipe a circle for nest

1. Using the green buttercream, rotate a cupcake in your hand as you add a ring of leaves around the edge of the cupcake. (See A.)

2. Use the brown buttercream to pipe a ring around the cupcake that sits on the edge of the leaves. (See B.) Continue to pipe more buttercream, adding another layer to build up the nest. (See C.)

3. Fill the nest with some toasted coconut. (See D.) Add a couple of jelly beans to the nest for the eggs. (See E.)

(E) add jelly beans to nest

Weddings

UNIT 8

I WENT INTO THE PASTRY BUSINESS because I wanted to make wedding cakes. That was thirteen years ago, and the wedding cakes are still a huge part of my business. During those years cupcake shops started popping up everywhere and I kept thinking the trend would slow, but each year we are doing more and more cupcakes for weddings and showers. Cupcakes are such sweet little treats, plus they are portable and economical. In this unit you will learn to make tiered wedding cupcakes, monogram cupcakes, shot glass cupcakes (for a dessert table or shower), and mason jar cupcakes (for a wedding favor).

Tiered Wedding Cupcakes

- jumbo cupcakes
- regular cupcakes
- vanilla buttercream (see recipe on page 133) in a 14"–18" (36–46 cm) pastry bag fitted with a large round tip such as Ateco #806
- vanilla buttercream in a 12" (30 cm) pastry bag fitted with a small #5 round tip
- sugar flowers
- toothpicks
- edible sugar pearls

These cupcakes are inspired by a traditional wedding cake, and they are a nice alternative to the individual cakes we often see at weddings. You could serve one per couple, or package them as a favor in a clear box.

Tip

Be sure to tell your guests there is a toothpick inside the cupcake. They should notice it when they peel the wrapper, but it is best to be safe.

Let's Go!

(A) place toothpick halfway into bottom of regular size cupcake

(C) pipe buttercream on top

(B) secure smaller cupcake to larger with toothpick

(D) add a small beaded border

1. Using the large round tip, pipe a single layer buttercream swirl on top of a jumbo cupcake.

2. Insert a toothpick halfway into the bottom of a regular size cupcake. (See A.) Place the regular size cupcake on top of the jumbo cupcake, pushing the toothpick into the buttercream and cake. (See B.)

3. Pipe a swirl of buttercream on top of the regular size cupcake. (See C.)

4. Add a small beaded border with the small round tip around the edge of the larger cupcake and the base of the smaller cupcake. (See D.)

5. Garnish with sugar pearls and a sugar flower, if desired.

You'll Need

- frosted cupcakes
- colored fondant (yellow and white shown)
- cornstarch
- luster dust
- small fondant roller
- fluted round cookie or biscuit cutters: 2¼", 1¾" (5.5, 4.5 cm)
- monogram stamp
- small paintbrush

A monogram typically consists of two or three letters, but more and more often we are seeing only one letter used in designs for weddings and parties. The monogram is often used for invitations, napkins, linens, signage, and dessert decor. In this lab you will learn how to combine a few fondant techniques into one sweet cupcake.

Tip

Use bright colors and include all letters of the alphabet for a baby shower or first birthday party. Buy an alphabet stamp in a playful font.

Let's Go!

1. Roll out the yellow fondant ¼" (6 mm) thick. See Lab 11 (page 34) for details on rolling out fondant. Use the larger round cutter to cut out fondant disks.

2. Roll out the white fondant. Press the monogram stamp into the fondant. (See A and B.)

3. Using the smaller cutter, center the cutter on the monogram and cut out the disk. (See C.)

4. Brush the larger disk with water. (See D.) Center the monogram disk on the larger disk. (See E.) Brush with luster dust if desired, or outline with royal icing.

5. Let fondant disks dry for a few hours. Place the disks on top of the cupcakes.

(A) press stamp into fondant

(B) stamp impression

(D) brush larger disk with water

(C) cut out monogram disk

(E) glue disks together

Shot Glass Tiramisu

- mini vanilla cupcakes
- mascarpone cream (see recipe below) in 12" (30 cm) pastry bag fitted with large round tip, such as Ateco #804
- Kahlúa syrup
- chocolate shavings
- cocoa powder
- shot glasses

Dessert tables are very popular for weddings. We typically make a smaller wedding cake, and then create eight to ten different varieties of bite size desserts. I like to use shot glasses with demitasse spoons for pots de créme, mousse, and mini cupcakes. These tiramisu shot glasses look sophisticated and taste amazing!

Tips

- To make mascarpone cream, mix equal parts cream cheese buttercream frosting (see recipe on page 133) and mascarpone. If the cream is too sweet for you, add more mascarpone.
- To make Kahlúa syrup, add two parts simple syrup to one part Kahlúa.

Let's Go!

1. Squirt mascarpone cream into the bottom of a shot glass. (See A.)

2. Remove the mini cupcake liner and place a cupcake on top of the cream. (See B.)

3. Brush the top of the cupcake generously with Kahlúa syrup. It is fine if some syrup drips down the sides of the cupcake. (See C.)

4. Pipe another dollop of mascarpone cream on top. (See D.)

5. Garnish with chocolate shavings and cocoa powder, if desired. (See E.)

Taking it Further

If you do not want to use shot glasses, this makes a great filled cupcake. Keep the cupcake in the wrapper and fill the center of the cupcake with the mascarpone cream. Proceed with step 3. Frost with mocha buttercream (page 84).

(A) add cream to shot glass

(B) place cupcake on top of cream

(D) top with mocha buttercream

(C) brush cupcake with syrup

(E) add garnish

ᴘʙᴊ Mason Jars

You'll Need

- vanilla cupcakes (see recipe on page 140)
- jam (raspberry shown)
- peanut butter buttercream (see recipe below)
- chopped peanuts
- 4" (10 cm) offset spatula
- mason jars

Mason jars filled with treats make great favors for a shower, rustic wedding, or a birthday party. Children (and adults) will love these peanut butter and jelly cupcakes. And you can reuse the jar!

Tips

- To make peanut butter buttercream, mix peanut butter into vanilla butter-cream (see recipe on page 133) to taste.
- Attach a ribbon and tag. This is a fabulous favor for an outdoor party.
- We iced the cupcakes with an offset spatula to give it a more rustic look, but you can use a piping bag if it's easier for you.

Let's Go!

(A) add jam to jar

(B) place cupcake in jar

1. Spread jam in the bottom of a jar. (See A.)

2. Center a cupcake in the jar on top of the jam. (See B.)

3. Top the cupcake with peanut butter buttercream. (See C.)

4. Sprinkle generously with chopped peanuts. (See D.)

(C) frost the cupcake

(D) sprinkle with peanuts

Taking it Further

For a trifle-style dessert in a mason jar, break two cupcakes into 1" (2.5 cm) pieces and layer jam, cake, and frosting until the mason jar is filled completely.

Cupcakes
with a Twist

IN THIS UNIT YOU WILL LEARN how to make some nontraditional cupcakes, such as cheesecake cupcakes and rich flourless chocolate cupcakes. And you will discover some fun trendy desserts such as cupcake push pops and cake truffles. These are all impressive desserts that will wow your friends.

UNIT

9

Cheesecake Cupcakes

- 1¾" (4.5 cm) round cookies, such as vanilla wafers or gingersnaps
- vanilla cheesecake batter (see recipe on page 139)
- fresh raspberries
- lemon curd (see recipe on page 142)
- sugar flowers or additional raspberries for garnish
- cupcake liners
- cupcake pan
- small ice cream scoop
- 4" (10 cm) offset spatula or small spoon

My mom made a version of these cupcakes when I was growing up and they were a staple at all our family parties. She used Nilla Wafers as the bottom crust and cherry pie filling as the topping. This is an updated version of that recipe using tangy lemon curd and fresh raspberries. A sweet sugar flower is the perfect adornment.

Homemade Bottom Crust

Make your own bottom crusts with your favorite sugar cookie recipe. Roll out the cookie dough ½" (1.3 cm) thick. Use a 1¾" (4.5 cm) round cutter, and cut out a couple dozen rounds; bake. Freeze remaining rounds for a later use in an airtight baggie or plastic container.

Let's Go!

1. Place the cupcake liners in the cupcake pan. Place one round cookie in the bottom of each liner. (See A.)

2. Using the ice cream scoop, place one scoop of cheesecake batter in each liner. (See B.)

3. Press a raspberry in the center of each scoop and top with additional batter, filling the liner three-quarters full. (See C.)

4. Bake at 300°F (150°C, or gas mark 2) for 20–30 minutes, or until just set in the center. (See D.) Let cool; chill.

5. Spread a thin layer of lemon curd on top of each cupcake with a spatula or small spoon. (See E.)

6. Garnish with a daisy sugar flower or fresh raspberry. (See F.)

(A) place cookie in liner

(B) scoop batter into liner

(C) add raspberry and more batter

(D) bake until just set

(E) spread lemon curd on top

(F) garnish with sugar flower

LAB 47 Cake Truffles

You'll Need

- cake crumbs (lemon shown)
- buttercream (see recipe on page 133)
- tempered chocolate or candy melts (white shown), melted and kept warm
- sprinkles
- small scoop (#70)
- parchment or waxed paper-lined sheet tray
- toasted coconut (optional)

Cake balls and pops have been a trend for a few years now. I tend to prefer the cake ball version because they look like truffles, they can be elegantly packaged, and they are easier to display. If you want to make cake pops for a fun kids' party, just add a stick.

Tips

- In step 1 you can use a spoon to mix the crumbs and buttercream, but you want to make sure you don't smash the crumbs or the truffles will be very mushy inside. I prefer using my hands.

- When dipping cake balls or truffles, use a heating pad underneath the chocolate to keep it warm but not too hot.

- To make cake pops, dip a stick in chocolate, and then push the stick into a ball before chilling.

Let's Go!

1. Place the cake crumbs and toasted coconut (if desired) in a large bowl. Gradually add small dollops of buttercream while tossing the crumbs with your hands or a spoon.

2. Add just enough buttercream so that you can form a small ball that stays together. Do not over mix. (See A.)

3. Use a scoop to portion the balls, roll in your hands, and place on a tray. Chill the balls for a few hours until set. (See B.)

4. Toss the balls into the candy melts or melted chocolate and scoop out with a fork. (See C.) Tap the fork on the side of the bowl to remove excess chocolate. Place the balls on a parchment-lined sheet tray. (See D.)

5. If desired, add sprinkles while the melted candy or chocolate is still wet. (See E.)

Taking It Further

- Once cake balls are set, drizzle them with a different type of chocolate.
- Try mixing toasted coconut into the cake batter.

(A) stop mixing when you can form a small ball

(B) scoop the balls and roll in hands

(C) coat balls in chocolate

(D) place on sheet tray

(E) add sprinkles

Cake Push Pops

- ½" (1.3 cm)-thick layers of cake (lemon cake shown)

- jam (strawberry shown) in a 12" (30 cm) pastry bag with a large round tip, such as Ateco #804

- flavored buttercream (see recipe on page 133; strawberry shown) in a 12" (30 cm) pastry bag with a large round tip, such as Ateco #804

- sprinkles or edible confetti

- 2" (5 cm) round cookie or biscuit cutter

- push pop containers

Cake Push Pops are new and trendy! They are the perfect portable treat and can be filled with many flavor combinations. You do have to buy the containers, but you can reuse them and there are lots of fun ways they can be displayed.

Tip

Mini cupcakes also fit in push pop containers. You will only be able to fit two cupcakes per pop with one layer of filling in between. You could slice the cupcakes in half horizontally if more filling is desired. You can fill these with any combination of jam, curd, ganache, or frosting.

Let's Go!

1. Cut cake layers into 2" (5 cm) rounds with a round cookie or biscuit cutter. Place one round in the bottom of the push pop container. (See A.)

2. Squeeze a thin layer of jam on top of the cake layer. (See B.)

3. Repeat with an additional cake layer. (See C.)

4. Squeeze a thin layer of buttercream on top of the cake layer. (See D.)

5. Top with a third cake layer, and finish with more buttercream. (See E and F.)

6. Garnish with sprinkles.

(A) place cake round in bottom of container

(B) add layer of jam

(C) add another cake layer

(D) add buttercream

(E) add third cake layer

(F) finish with buttercream

- nonstick spray
- cupcake batter (vanilla cardamom batter shown)
- rose water glaze (see recipe below)
- edible rose petals
- egg white
- superfine sugar
- mini cake mold (rose bundt cake mold or design of your choice)
- metal rack
- sheet pan

A cupcake can be baked in many shapes. We baked our vanilla cupcake batter (with a small amount of cardamom added for a kick) in mini rose-shaped bundt pans and drizzled them with rose-water glaze. Candied rose petals are a lovely garnish.

Tips

- To make rose water glaze, whisk together ½ cup (60 g) powdered sugar and 2–3 tablespoons (30–45 ml) heavy cream. Add rose water to taste (less than 1 tablespoon [15 ml]).
- In step 2 you can scrape up and reuse excess glaze.

Let's Go!

(A) *bake cupcake batter in bundt mold*

(C) *add more glaze*

(B) *drizzle with glaze*

(D) *rub petals to remove excess sugar*

1. To make bundt cakes, first spray the mold with nonstick spray. Fill the mold three-quarters full, and bake until a toothpick comes out clean; 20–25 minutes. Let cakes cool five minutes in the pan, and then turn them out onto a sheet pan. (See A.)

2. Place bundts on a metal rack over a sheet pan; drizzle with glaze. (See B and C.)

3. Refer to Lab 9 (page 28) for candied flowers. Paint the flower petals with egg white and sprinkle with superfine sugar. Rub the petals lightly with your fingers to remove excess sugar. (See D.)

- flourless chocolate cake batter (see recipe on page 139)
- ganache (see recipe on page 135)
- raspberry jam in pastry bag fitted with #3 round tip
- raspberries
- porcelain ramekins or silicone cupcake molds
- roasting pan; any pan with 2" (5 cm) sides will work
- metal rack
- sheet pan

Flourless chocolate cakes have been on restaurant dessert menus for years, and I still love them. They are not difficult to make, but they look chic and taste indulgent. They are a wonderful gluten-free option, too.

Tips

- To avoid getting water in your cake batter when putting the pan in the oven, place the roasting pan with filled molds on the oven rack, and then carefully pour hot water into the pan before closing the oven door.
- Vary your plate—try caramel sauce, crème anglaise, white chocolate, or an orange jam.

Let's Go!

(A) *place cakes in water bath in roasting pan*

(B) *flip cakes onto rack*

(D) *use spatula to fill gaps*

1. To bake chocolate cakes, fill ramekins or molds three-quarters full with cake batter, and place in a roasting pan. Pour hot water into the pan until it reaches halfway up the sides of the molds. (See A.)

2. Bake at 300°F (150°C, or gas mark 2) until just set in center; 20–25 minutes. Let cakes cool completely, and then flip them out onto a rack. (See B.)

3. Place cakes on the metal rack over a sheet pan. Coat each cake with ganache to cover. (See C.) To ensure sides are coated, use an offset spatula to quickly spread ganache into gaps. (See D.) Let the cakes set. Scrape up the remaining ganache from the sheet tray and reserve for another use.

4. Pipe jam onto a plate using a pastry bag. Remove a cake from the rack and place on the plate. (See E.) Garnish with raspberries.

(C) *coat with ganache*

(E) *remove from rack onto garnished plates*

Presentation

PRESENTATION IS A VERY IMPORTANT PART of any dessert. The look of the dessert itself is critical, and so are its surroundings. A simply frosted cupcake can look fabulous with the right paper liner, packaging, or placement on an ornately decorated dessert table. Cupcakes also make great gifts, but you must have the right packaging. I love searching antique stores, discount stores, and clearance racks for cake stands, platters, and pedestals to add to my collection.

UNIT

10

Pedestals & Cupcake Stands

- cupcakes
- pedestals
- decorative plates and platters
- cupcake stands
- decorative glassware

When displaying cupcakes I very rarely use one huge cupcake tower. I like to use a smaller cupcake stand mixed with various pedestals and platters. If you have time to make other desserts or buy some candy, it will make the table much more festive.

Tip

Fill glass jars or vases with fruits, fun straws, rock candy, lollipops, or licorice, to give some height to your dessert table.

Let's Go!

1. Cupcake towers are trendy and are often a replacement for the traditional wedding cake. However, we don't recommend putting the "cutting" cake on the top tier. There is a reason the bride and groom don't cut the top tier of a wedding cake—it is very awkward reaching up that high. We recommend placing the "cutting" cake on a separate beautiful pedestal so people focus on this special little cake, and the bride and groom can cut it easily. (See A.)

(A) cutting cake

2. Dessert tables are a huge trend right now for weddings, birthday parties, and other events. They look adorable and add stylish decor to your room with delicious cupcakes and other sweets. It is best to have a theme, color palette, and focal point—such as a cake or cupcake stand from which you design your table. Using various heights is essential to a fabulous table, and handmade signs give it a personal touch. (See B.)

3. Don't be afraid to mix different styles of pedestals, cake stands, and platters. Create a bright, wild display with lots of color and texture, or a sleek modern display with glass, silver, and white.

(B) dessert table

You'll Need

- cupcake boxes with inserts
- cellophane bags
- 12 oz (355 ml) clear plastic cups and lids
- Chinese take-out boxes
- cupcake wraps
- cupcake kits

Cupcakes are not easy to package because they are fragile and can topple over if not secured. There are some really cute boxes and bags available online and in craft stores. Below are some new ideas and tips for packaging.

cupcake kits

Tip

Cupcake kits are readily available and they include coordinating liners and toppers. This is a great way to match your cupcakes to your theme when you are short on time.

Let's Go!

(A) *box with inserts*

1. Use cupcake inserts, or line the cupcakes up against each other in boxes so they do not slide in transit. (See A.)

2. For a party favor, use a clear cupcake box, or a clear cellophane bag with a ribbon. The bag is best for fondant-covered cupcakes because butter-cream can stick to the bag. (See B.)

3. At our bakery we often put individual cupcakes in an upside down 12 oz (355 ml) cup with a lid—it's portable and you can reuse the cup! (See C.)

4. Chinese take-out boxes come in all different colors, including clear. They are another great packaging option. (See D.)

5. Cupcake wraps are becoming very popular. Make your own by creating a template and using craft scissors and punches, or purchase them at most craft stores and online. (See E.)

(B) *clear bag with cupcake*

(C) *cupcake in cup*

(D) *Chinese take-out box*

(E) *cupcake wraps*

Favorite Recipes

BAKING CAN BE INTIMIDATING, ESPECIALLY FROM SCRATCH. Of course you can use cupcake mixes and premade frostings for any of the labs presented, but I hope you are inspired by the recipes and will give scratch baking a try. I am a true believer in using quality, fresh, and, if possible, local ingredients. I have included some essential but simple recipes that we use everyday at the bakery. Be sure to try our signature Swiss meringue buttercream. It is light, fluffy, and not too sweet. Enjoy!

Swiss Meringue Buttercream

Swiss meringue is a classic buttercream frosting. *This is my go-to recipe for buttercream and should be used for all the labs unless otherwise noted.* I have tweaked the proportions over the years, but I learned how to work with this buttercream at my first baking job in Chicago. The owner decorated wedding cakes with this frosting, which is rare. It is not as stable as Italian meringue but it tastes amazing. It is light, not too sweet, and very easy to make. It is the only buttercream I use, and I have many clients that exclaim, "This is the best frosting I have ever had!" It needs to be at room temperature to enjoy, because it is hard like butter when chilled. The buttercream will melt like butter too, so it's important to keep your cupcakes chilled before transport or on a hot day.

8 ounces (235 ml) egg whites

1½ cup sugar (300 g)

1 pound (450 g) soft butter, cut into 2" (5 cm) chunks

1 teaspoon (5 ml) vanilla extract

1. Whisk egg whites and sugar in a large stainless bowl over a hot water bath until hot to the touch and the sugar is dissolved; 140°F (60°C) on an instant-read thermometer. Be sure to whisk the mixture constantly or the egg whites will cook over the heat.

2. Whip mixture to stiff peaks with a hand mixer, or use the whisk attachment on a stand mixer.

3. Add the softened butter piece by piece, and then the vanilla. Scrape down the sides of the bowl and mix on medium speed until the buttercream comes together.

4. Store buttercream in an airtight container in the refrigerator for one week, or in the freezer for up to three months.

Yield: About 4 cups (940 ml), enough to frost 12 cupcakes

Tips

- The buttercream may look separated before it reaches a smooth, shiny consistency. You cannot over-mix this buttercream; just mix it until it looks smooth.

- If you see lumps of butter, your butter was too cold. Place the bowl over a double boiler, melt slightly, and then rewhip. If your buttercream looks smooth but is very liquid, it is too warm. Chill the bowl for 5–10 minutes; rewhip.

Cream Cheese Buttercream

This is a delicious frosting, essential for carrot and red velvet cake. Not too sweet; nice and tangy.

8 ounces (225 g) cream cheese, soft

8 ounces (225 g) unsalted butter, soft

1 teaspoon (5 ml) vanilla extract

2¼ cup (270 g) powdered sugar, sifted

1. Place cream cheese in a large bowl or the bowl of a stand mixer. Beat until smooth, scraping down the sides as needed.

2. Slowly add the butter until incorporated and smooth, scraping down the sides as needed.

3. Add vanilla. Slowly add powdered sugar. Once all of the sugar is added, scrape down the sides, increase speed to medium, and beat for 1 minute or until smooth.

4. Store in refrigerator for one week.

Yield: About 3 cups (700 ml), enough to frost 12 cupcakes

Fruit Glaze

This is a nice natural glaze for cupcakes. We use seasonal fruits and make all our own purees at the bakery. Puree the fruit in the blender (a mixture of fruits is delicious too). Then cook down the puree with some sugar to reduce the liquid. Freeze the puree in small portions, and then you can pull out the puree as needed to make the glaze.

12 ounces (340 g) powdered sugar (approximately 3 cups [360 g])
¼–⅓ cup (60–80 ml) fruit puree (raspberry, strawberry, orange, etc.)

1. Combine all ingredients in a large bowl or the bowl of a stand mixer.
2. Beat or whisk slowly until the powdered sugar starts to mix in. If using an electric mixer increase speed to medium, or beat by hand until icing is smooth and shiny; about 3 minutes. Add more or less puree as needed to reach consistency needed for topping cupcakes.

Yield: About 2 cups (470 ml)

Ganache

Rich, creamy ganache is an essential recipe for all bakers and pastry chefs. It is versatile and can be whipped, piped, poured, or molded, depending on it's consistency. Don't skimp on the chocolate—a high quality chocolate yields a great tasting ganache.

1 cup (235 ml) heavy cream
8 ounces (225 g) chopped dark or semi-sweet chocolate
pinch of salt

1. Heat cream until it simmers or bubbles around the edges.
2. Place chopped chocolate in a large bowl—a stainless steel bowl is ideal. Pour hot cream over the chocolate. Cover with plastic wrap for 3–5 minutes until the chocolate melts; add salt.
3. Whisk mixture to combine. If chocolate chunks still remain, rewarm the mixture over a double boiler.
4. Let cool.
5. Store the ganache by pressing a piece of plastic wrap onto the ganache surface so a film does not form on top; let sit at room temperature for two days. Refrigerate ganache for a longer shelf life.

Yield: 1¾ cups (425 ml)

Tip

Ganache can be infused with flavors. Add herbs to the cream, such as lavender or mint. Strain the herbs before adding the cream to the chocolate. You can also add flavorings to the finished ganache, such as liqueurs, instant espresso powder, extracts, and fruit purees.

Royal Icing

Royal icing is simple to make and essential for decorations that you want to dry hard. It is the only icing we use for sugar cookies to give a nice shiny, bright finish. In this book, we note the consistency of royal icing you will need. Stiff peaks are best for detailed piping and flowers. Medium peaks are best for outlining and basic piping. Liquid icing with no peaks is best for filling in run-outs or sugar cookies.

3 egg whites

4½ cups (560 g) powdered sugar

1 tablespoon (15 ml) water

1. Combine all ingredients in a large bowl or the bowl of a stand mixer. Beat or whisk slowly until the powdered sugar begins to mix in. If you use an electric mixer, increase the speed to medium, or beat by hand until the icing is smooth and shiny; about 3 minutes.
2. Adjust the amount of sugar or water to reach the desired consistency.

Yield: About 2 cups (470 ml)

Chocolate Cupcakes

3 cups (360 g) all-purpose flour

1 teaspoon baking powder

1 teaspoon baking soda

1 teaspoon salt

¾ cup (210 g) dark or Dutch cocoa powder

¾ cup (180 ml) hot water

2¼ cups (400 g) sugar

4 eggs

1½ cups (355 ml) canola oil

1 tablespoon vanilla

1 cup (240 ml) buttermilk

1. Preheat oven to 350°F (180°C, or gas mark 4).
2. Sift flour, baking powder, baking soda, and salt together in a medium bowl.
3. In a small bowl, whisk together the hot water and cocoa powder together until no lumps remain.
4. Combine the sugar and eggs in a large mixing bowl or stand mixer with the whisk. Add oil and vanilla.
5. Add cocoa mixture to sugar mixture gradually, whisking constantly.
6. Alternate adding the dry ingredients with the buttermilk in three parts, beginning and ending with dry.
7. Divide batter into cupcake paper liners. Bake 16–20 minutes.

Yield: 35–40 cupcakes

Flourless Chocolate Cake

Flourless chocolate cakes are the ultimate dessert for chocolate lovers, and they can be garnished with so many different options. If you are intimidated by glazing the cupcakes with ganache, simply dust them with powdered sugar and drizzle with ganache instead.

16 ounces (455 g) semi-sweet chocolate, chopped

½ pound (2 sticks, 225 g) unsalted butter

1 tablespoon (15 ml) vanilla

8 eggs

¼ cup (50 g) sugar

½ teaspoon (2.5 g) salt

1. Preheat the oven to 300°F (150°C, or gas mark 2).
2. Melt the chocolate and butter over a water bath until smooth; stir in vanilla. Let the mixture cool slightly while you beat the eggs.
3. Using a stand or hand mixer, beat the eggs, sugar, and salt on high speed until volume doubles in size—about 5 minutes.
4. Using a spatula, fold one-third of the egg mixture into the chocolate until the eggs are almost fully incorporated. Repeat by folding in half of the remaining mixture, and then the last third until the batter is completely mixed together.
5. For smaller cakes see the directions in Lab 50 on page 124. To make a larger cake, line an 8" or 9" (20–23 cm) springform pan with parchment paper on the bottom. Spread the batter into the prepared pan and tap on the counter to smooth the surface. Wrap the bottom of spring form pan in foil so water does not leak in. Place in larger roasting pan and pour hot water in the pan around the springform pan. Bake until the cake has risen slightly and the center is almost set, similar to cheesecake; 20–25 minutes for cupcakes, 25–30 minutes for 8" (20 cm) pan, and 18–20 minutes for 9" (23 cm) pan.
6. Remove the pan from the water bath and set on a rack to cool.

Cover and refrigerate 4–6 hours before releasing the cake from the pan. The cake can be stored two to three days in the refrigerator.

Yield: 12 cupcakes or ramekins, or one 8" or 9" (20–23 cm) round cake

Vanilla Cheesecake

I use this recipe for cheesecake cupcakes, bars, and full-size cheesecakes. It has a nice creamy texture and works wonderfully in the lemon raspberry cupcakes on page 139. For a chocolate cheesecake cupcake, add a few ounces of melted chocolate to the batter before baking and top with ganache instead of lemon curd.

16 ounces (450 g) cream cheese at room temperature

1 cup (200 g) sugar

3 eggs

1 teaspoon (5 ml) vanilla

¼ cup (60 ml) heavy cream

1. Preheat the oven to 325°F (170°C, or gas mark 3). Place cupcake liners in muffin pan and then add a cookie for the bottom crust.
2. Cream the cream cheese and sugar together until smooth (no lumps).
3. Add eggs one at a time, scraping down the sides of the bowl.
4. Add vanilla and cream; beat.
5. Scoop into muffin cups and bake 18–20 minutes.

Yield: About 12 cupcakes

Vanilla Cupcakes

This moist and delicious cupcake recipe can be adjusted for a variety of flavors. Simply stir the seasoning ingredients into the batter before baking. Try lemon zest and lemon juice for lemon cupcakes, or coconut flakes for coconut cupcakes. Orange zest is fresh and wonderful too. After baking, brush the tops with flavored syrup or fill the baked vanilla cupcakes with jam, pastry cream, or lemon curd. So many options, all of them delicious.

1½ cups (190 g) cake flour or all-purpose flour

½ teaspoon (2.5 g) baking powder

¼ teaspoon (1.2 g) baking soda

½ teaspoon (2.5 g) salt

6 ounces (1½ sticks [168 g]) unsalted butter, room temperature

1 cup (200 g) sugar

3 eggs

1 teaspoon (5 ml) vanilla

½ cup (120 ml) buttermilk

1. Preheat the oven to 350°F (180°C, or gas mark 4).
2. Sift flour, baking powder, baking soda, and salt together in a medium bowl; set aside.
3. In the bowl of an electric mixer fitted with the paddle attachment (or use hand mixer), beat the butter and sugar until light and fluffy, about 3 minutes, and scraping down the sides as needed.
4. Add eggs one at a time, scraping down the sides in between additions, and mixing on low speed until incorporated; add vanilla.
5. Alternate adding the dry ingredients with the buttermilk in three parts, beginning and ending with dry.
6. Divide batter into cupcake paper liners. Bake 15–18 minutes.

Yield: 18–20 cupcakes

Tip

I prefer cake flour for a more tender cupcake, but the cakes will still be delicate with all-purpose flour.

White Chocolate Truffle Mix

Chocolate truffles look fancy and are often intimidating to make, but they don't have to be. It can be tricky to dip them in tempered chocolate, so instead we rolled these in coconut to make the snowmen. To showcase them in a different way, try rolling in chopped nuts, cocoa powder, sprinkles, or chocolate shavings. This truffle mixture can be used without the coconut too. Add a little liqueur for a flavor boost.

¼ cup (60 ml) heavy cream

8 ounces (225 g) good quality white chocolate, finely chopped

¼ cup (26 g) finely shredded sweetened coconut

1. In a small saucepan, bring the cream to a simmer.
2. Remove the pan from the heat, stir in chocolate, and whisk until smooth.
3. Transfer the mixture to a bowl and stir in the coconut.
4. Refrigerate until firm enough to scoop and roll into balls.

Yield: About 1 cup (295 g); makes about 20 (½ ounce [15 g]) truffles.

Lime Curd

1 stick (8 tablespoons [120 g]) unsalted butter

1 egg

6 egg yolks

1 cup (200 g) sugar

zest of 3 limes

1/3 cup (80 ml) lime juice

1½ tablespoons (12 g) cornstarch, dissolved in cold water

1. Melt butter over low heat in a small- or medium-size stainless steel heavy-bottom stock pot. Let cool a few minutes.

2. In a separate bowl, whisk together egg, egg yolks, and sugar.

3. Whisk in lime zest and juice.

4. Whisk lime mixture and cornstarch into the melted butter to combine.

5. Place over low heat and stir constantly with a heat-proof rubber spatula.

6. Bring to a boil in saucepan and boil for one complete minute, stirring constantly. Strain with a fine mesh strainer to remove the zest and any cooked egg bits. Chill before using.

Tip: For lemon curd, replace lime zest and lime juice with lemon.

Sugar Cookies

3¼ cups (400 g) all-purpose flour

¼ teaspoon salt

2½ sticks (20 tablespoons [300 g]) unsalted butter, room temperature

1 cup (200 g) granulated sugar

1 large egg

1 large egg yolk

1 teaspoon vanilla extract

1. Preheat oven to 350°F (180°C, or gas mark 4).

2. In a medium bowl, whisk together flour and salt.

3. In a large bowl, cream butter and sugar with a hand or stand mixer on medium-high until light and creamy, scraping down the sides with a spatula to smooth any lumps.

4. Add egg, egg yolk, and vanilla, and mix on low until incorporated, scraping the sides.

5. Slowly add flour mixture, 1/3 at a time, mixing on low until evenly combined.

6. Divide dough into 2 discs, 1–2 inches (2 ½–5 cm) thick, wrap in plastic wrap, and refrigerate until firm, at least 1 hour. Dough can be made 3–4 days in advance, or frozen for up to 6 months. Raw cookie cut-outs can be frozen too.

7. On a lightly floured surface, roll cookies to ¼ inch (⅔ cm) thick. Use cookie cutters to cut into shapes. Spread cookies ½ inch (1¼ cm) apart on cookie sheets.

8. Bake cookies until golden brown on edges, 10 to 15 minutes, depending on size of cookie. Cool on cooling rack. Decorate as desired.

Resources

AC Moore

www.acmoore.com

full line of baking and decorating supplies

BRP Box Shop

www.brpboxshop.com

cupcake boxes & inserts

Fancy Flours

www.fancyflours.com

baking cups, edible decorations, wafer paper, cookie cutters

Global Sugar Art

www.globalsugarart.com

fondant, gumpaste, fondant & gumpaste tools, silicone molds, impression mats, edible decorations, cupcake & cake pans

Hobby Lobby

www.hobbylobby.com

full line of baking and decorating supplies

Jo-Ann Fabrics & Crafts

www.joann.com

full line of baking and decorating supplies

King Arthur Flour

www.kingarthurflour.com

ingredients, baking pans, cookie cutters, baking tools

Michaels

www.michaels.com

full line of baking and decorating supplies

Paper Mart

www.papermart.com

packaging supplies, ribbons, bows, tissue paper, boxes, cellophane bags, take-out boxes

Wilton

www.wilton.com

full line of baking and decorating supplies

About the Author

Bridget Cavanaugh Thibeault, chef/co-proprietor with John Emerman and Tatyana Rehn of Luna Bakery & Cafe in Cleveland Heights, Ohio, began her career in advertising in Chicago after earning a degree from Marquette University. A love for cooking and creativity led her to culinary school where she earned an associates of applied science degree in culinary arts from the Cooking & Hospitality Institute of Chicago.

Bridget moved to New York City to become a food stylist, gaining experience in both print and television for major food brands and publications. Flour Girl, her custom cake and dessert business, was launched as a creative side business. She returned to Chicago in 2004 to work as culinary director at a culinary consulting firm doing recipe and menu development, testing, writing, product ideation, and food styling.

In 2006, Bridget relocated to her hometown of Cleveland to focus on her growing Flour Girl business, which in turn led to her partnership with John and Tatyana. In 2011 they opened Luna Bakery & Cafe. Luna offers fresh breakfast, lunch, and dinner options including crepes, salads, paninis, local espresso, and coffee. Specialities include: made-from-scratch pastries, cupcakes, and wedding cakes. To learn more about Luna visit www.lunabakerycafe.com.

Acknowledgments

I would like to thank ...

Scott Mievogel at Easywind Studio for the beautiful photography.

Mary Ann Hall, Marla Stefanelli, and everyone at Quarry for this fun opportunity.

Brynn Keefe for her crafty styling, Caitlin Reynolds for her handy work, and Sarah Keller for her enthusiastic assistance.

My partners, John Emerman and Tatyana Rehn, for letting me take on this venture in the first year of our booming little café—and everyone at Luna for their talent and dedication.

My wonderful husband and supporter, Marc, and our adorable son, Cavan, who kept me laughing and smiling through all the long days.